Initiatives for Mission
1980-2002

UNITED METHODIST CHURCH

HISTORY OF MISSION SERIES

Initiatives for Mission 1980–2002

CHARLES E. COLE, EDITOR

GENERAL BOARD OF GLOBAL MINISTRIES
The United Methodist Church
New York, New York

Copyright © 2003
The General Board of Global Ministries
The United Methodist Church
475 Riverside Drive
New York, New York 10115

All rights reserved.
Permissions information listed on page 135
Printed in the United States of America

LIBRARY OF CONGRESS
Control Number 2002117827

ISBN 1-890569-61-5 CLOTH
ISBN 1-890569-77-1 PAPER

COVER PHOTOS *(left to right from top left)*:
Chicuque, Mozambique, hospital; Tallinn Center,
Estonia; children in Honduras; J. Edward Carothers;
Zambia health worker; Randolph W. Nugent;
Russian man and child; UMW Assembly.

[Contents]

List of Illustrations, vii
Foreword, ix

Introduction
  F. Herbert Skeete, 1

1. **A Journey of Amazing Grace**
   Ann Rader Pfisterer (1981–1984), 7

2. **The Origin and Creation of a Theology of Mission Statement**
   Betty S. Gordon (1981–1988), 25

3. **A Servant People to God's Creation**
   Woodrow Hearn (1989–1992), 39

4. **Years of Initiative for Mission**
   F. Herbert Skeete (1993–1996), 55

5. **Mission Is Incarnation**
   Dan E. Solomon (1997–2000), 63

6. **Endowed by God**
   Arthur F. Kulah (1993–2000), 75

7. **Developing a Culture of Mutuality: The Central Conference of Central and Southern Europe as a Partner in Mission**
   Heinrich Bolleter (1993–2000), 81

8. **Visions Shaping the Future**
   Arturo Fernandez (1993–2000), 89

9. **Witnessing to the Gospel in Word and Deed**
   Jenni Yeoh (1993–2000), 101

10. **Fifty Years after the Universal Declaration of Human Rights: A Latin American and Caribbean Perspective**
    Frederico J. Pagura, Argentina (1998), 107

11. **Mission: A Commitment to Action**
    Joel Martinez (2000–2002), 113

Notes, 129

Permissions, 135

Index, 137

[Photographs]

Randolph W. Nugent, p. xiv
J. Edward Carothers, p. 15
Pittsburgh Consultation, p. 29
Russian man and child, p. 44
Chicuque Hospital, p. 53
Goma Refugees, p. 58
Cambodia, p. 67
Angola mine victims, p. 69
Bishop Kulah, Liberia, p. 78
Tallinn Center, p. 86
Honduras relief, p. 99
Zambia health worker, p. 103
Plaza de Mayo *Abuelas*, p. 109
Ground Zero, p. 115
Women's Assembly, p. 121

[Foreword]

More than fifty years have passed since a history of mission series was begun by The Methodist Church Board of Missions. Wade Crawford Barclay wrote *Early American Methodism, 1769–1844* as the first of what would become a four-volume series.

In that first volume, Barclay explained that the series was "designed to present a comprehensive, detailed, and accurate history of American Methodism in its character as a Christian missionary movement." He laid out the publishing program as including the content of volume one, early American Methodism, and then the mission histories of the three divisions of mainstream Methodism prior to 1939: the Methodist Episcopal Church (MEC), the so-called northern church; the Methodist Episcopal Church, South (MECS), the so-called southern church; and the Methodist Protestant Church (MPC).

By the time of the third volume, however, Barclay was apologetic: "The writing of this volume has required more time than was anticipated." The second volume had brought the history only up to 1844, and that only of the MEC. The third volume advanced the MEC history to 1895. A fourth volume, written by J. Tremayne Copplestone after Barclay's death, completed the MEC mission work, ending in 1939. With the publication of this volume in 1973, however, the project stopped. The four volumes had taken a quarter century and the Board of Missions had by then evolved into the Board of Global Ministries of a new denomination, The United Methodist Church. The Board apparently felt the histories did not articulate an adequate vision of mission.

By the end of the twentieth century it seemed apparent to many that a continuation of the history of mission was needed. There were several reasons. The Women's Division almost alone in The UMC had continued to educate an important constituency about mission, supporting the National Council of Churches of Christ in its publication of annual mission resources and publishing many resources of its own. When the NCCC found it could no longer continue publishing these books, the Women's Division led the General Board of Global Ministries to continue their publication. The Women's Division more than most was conscientious in publishing works about mission. Yet many in the rest of the denomination remained untouched by any serious study of mission, present or past.

A second large reason consisted of the bridges that had flowed under the water since the conclusion of the Barclay/Copplestone series. The history of mission of The Methodist Church, in existence from 1939 to 1968, had never been written. The history of mission of the Evangelical United Brethren, in existence from 1946 to 1968, had never been written. Since these two merged to become The United Methodist Church, critical changes had occurred in the comprehension, strategy, and practice of mission in the newly united denomination. The very nature of the denominations had altered greatly in relation to the rest of the culture and in relation to the ecumenical movement. A need existed to write all these histories taking these changes into account. Furthermore, the MECS and MPC histories needed to be written and published.

A third reason lay in the religious and cultural changes that affected the way history is conceived and written. At the time Barclay began his series, women were almost totally absent from the official leadership of the mainline churches. African Americans, Hispanics, Asian Americans, and Native Americans were not well represented in that leadership. Bishops, officers of the major program boards like the Board of Missions of The Methodist Church, and other denominational officials consisted almost entirely of white men.

The need, then, was to develop a history of mission that did justice to the role of women, ethnic minorities in the United States, and also indigenous leaders in various countries. For most of the histories of mission previously published had ignored the leadership and contributions of indigenous leaders as well.

Finally, the field of history itself had changed. Chronicles of official events and even large-scale interpretations, or "metahistories," had given way to more detailed studies of local and culturally specific developments. "Thick description" was preferred to chronicles of facts and dates. Traditional histories are still being written, those that take a large field and attempt to provide an overriding image or concept for interpretation and those that relate personal histories. These efforts, while entertaining and even popular, eventually fail because of their biases, the inevitable inability of a single historian to know that large a field, or simply because they ignore the human race in its diversity.

This series might seem to be attempting such large-scale interpretations. Writers were advised to provide an interpretive framework while avoiding the attempt to create "repositories of facts." Instead, they were to "provide readable narratives" that would be placed "within the context of culture/religion interaction." We were keenly aware of the dangers of attempting histories "from the center," as it were, rather than "from the periphery," that is, from the perspective of previously neglected people. We hoped, however, that by breaking the histories into periods of fairly brief epochs and by seeking diligently to give voice to the voiceless inasmuch as the historical record allowed, we could fill the vacuum left in mission history since the conclusion of the Barclay/Copplestone series.

We hoped even more that we could produce histories that might be actually read by United Methodists and others committed to mission. This may seem an even more dubious undertaking, since the advent of electronic media has threatened to abolish reading entirely. Yet the increased publication of books and magazines because of the electronic media itself gives us some hope that reading may extend into the next generation.

The General Board of Global Ministries, through grants provided by the office of the general secretary, initiated the "United Methodist History of Mission" in 1999. It was conceived as a way to accomplish four goals:

1. To complete the outlines of the history of mission of The Methodist Church and its predecessors as given in *The History of Methodist Missions*, by Wade Crawford Barclay and J. Tremayne Copplestone.
2. To provide readable narratives or thematic treatments that can be used by both scholars and the general church membership.
3. To do justice to the contributions of women, ethnic minorities, and indigenous leaders to the history of mission.
4. To provide the basis for a video and other resources to be used in orienting GBGM staff and missionaries in our history.

This volume is one of a series that will consist of the following:

- the history of mission of the Methodist Protestant Church, 1830–1939
- the history of mission of the Methodist Episcopal Church, South, 1845–1939
- the history of mission of The Methodist Church, 1939–1968

- the history of mission of the Evangelical United Brethren Church, 1946–1968
- the history of mission of The United Methodist Church, 1968–2000
- reflections on Christian mission in the early decades of the third millennium of Christian history
- first-person accounts of presidents and directors of the United Methodist General Board of Global Ministries in undertaking significant mission initiatives from 1980 to 2002.

These histories are dedicated to past and present generations of Methodists, EUBs, and United Methodists who helped to fulfill the commitment "to reform the Continent and to spread scriptural Holiness over these lands." They are also offered in the hope that future generations will find in them not only information and interpretation of Christian mission but inspiration to continue that mission in the future. Although a reading of these histories will reveal failures as well as successes, contemporary Christians cannot but be grateful for the accomplishments of our foreparents in the faith. "We feebly struggle, they in glory shine."

Charles E. Cole, EDITOR

*Initiatives for Mission
1980–2002*

Randolph W. Nugent

[Introduction]

*W*HEN I SERVED in the Philadelphia Area, the conference treasurer, the Reverend Dale Owens, reported that a member of the United Methodist congregation he attended said to him: "At my canasta games we had a person who belongs to an independent congregation who was bragging about her church support of a missionary in South America. I was embarrassed that I could not share with her what my church was doing in mission." Dale then informed her that members of The United Methodist Church (UMC) do mission in covenant with each other through the General Board of Global Ministries (GBGM), which has nearly 2,000 missionaries and has mission work in universities, hospitals, clinics, day care centers, primary schools, community centers, and nursing homes in 160 countries across the globe.

The significant work of our General Board of Global Ministries should be shouted from every United Methodist pulpit and pew. Much of the sacrificial mission witness of our church becomes possible through the work of dedicated staff members of this Board. This book is a wonderful attempt to capture some of the outstanding and effective leadership of our Board, especially that of the general secretary, the Reverend Dr. Randolph W. Nugent.

In this book, the contributing authors will share the exciting missional journeys of GBGM in the years preceding and into the new millennium and celebrate the challenging and creative leadership of the Board. Dr. Nugent is also an historic first African-American United Methodist pastor to lead GBGM and our United Methodist Church in our mission witness in the world.

I have known Randy, as his friends call him, since the late 1950s when we were in seminary at Drew University. We were young pastors together in the New York East Annual Conference. Randy served as student pastor in Long Island City, Queens; I served in South Ozone Park, Queens; the Reverend Calvin Pressley assisted the Reverend William James in Harlem;

the Reverend John Carrington served in Springfield Gardens, Queens; and the Reverend Elemit Brooks served in the Bronx. These formed an invincible support group that helped in many difficult challenges along the way. We still continue to gather with our wives at least once a year around Christmas time and on other occasions when any one of the group calls. From this group has come outstanding leadership at all levels of the UMC.

Randy was the first of the group to serve outside of New York City. He accepted an appointment in the Troy Annual Conference, which was a part of the New York Episcopal Area. He served the First UMC in Albany. The rest of us remained in the New York East Annual Conference much longer. (The conference eventually became the New York Annual Conference.)

Randy was the only student at Drew University driving a Mercedes-Benz. It was an old model but it was a Mercedes. We knew then he had the potential to go on to higher leadership responsibilities. After graduation he has not owned a Mercedes to this day.

Another indication of his unusual gifts is his interest in the latest electronic or technical gadgets, especially those that can be incorporated into administrative or missional purposes. So when we sat with the bishops of Africa and heard of their challenges and the lack of communication with their colleagues within their areas and across the denomination, Randy's response came quickly: "We can take care of that." Shortly afterwards Randy had made available special wireless phones that would work on car batteries and hook into satellite transmission. These were available in Europe and Randy arranged for a pilot of The UMC in Europe to deliver these special phone units to the bishops in Africa.

Randy's preparation as a youth in New York City, as part of the first group of male students to enter a previously all-women's school at Hunter College, his pastoral experience in Long Island City, a difficult area of New York City, his mission in the Troy Annual Conference, his leadership with Metropolitan Urban Service Training (MUST), and his leadership contributions through the National Program Division and other sections of GBGM all helped produce one of the outstanding leaders of The UMC.

The fact that he became the first African American to lead the mission board of The UMC created as much constant pressure as the ever-evolving crises of the 1970s and 1980s. As bishops we endure the pressures of our areas and share with our colleagues the pressures outside our areas. For the general secretary of the largest and most diversified general board of our church, the pressure from all areas of the church in all the far reaches of the globe is overwhelming. There is no telling whence the next challenge can arise for the leadership of GBGM. Yet with amazing vision and patience, Randy has not only survived but has made a unique contribution to the missional witness of our church in the world.

The many chapters of this book will unfold the special blessings that GBGM has, in the name of The United Methodist Church, brought to thousands — even millions — of persons in the U.S. and around the world.

I was first elected to serve as a clergy member of GBGM in 1972. It was the year that the General Conference had restructured the boards and agencies of the church and had brought some unwilling groups kicking and screaming together under what some called a monstrosity of a Board. With them came some very strong administrative leaders, Randy included, and Dr. Tracey K. Jones, Jr., was given the challenge as general secretary to keep that newly formed ship afloat and moving.

I was assigned to the National Division and remained on the division for the second quadrennium, until 1980. During those eight years, I worked closely with Randy, who was the associate general secretary of the National Division under the leadership of Dr. Jones. I served as the chair of the Finance Committee during the second quadrennium.

The General Conference of 1972 had great difficulty in finding a satisfactory solution in reorganizing the boards and agencies of the church, as we are prone to do after a few years. I call it "moving the furniture around with little real change." We seem to find satisfaction in these games as United Methodists, with little concern for the costs both financially and missionally.

In the 1970s the mainline, predominantly white denominations were attacked from all sides of the ethnic spectrum. The National Division was the inevitable source of contact with the rest of The UMC, and Randy our leader was there to relate to the many evolving challenges that were being generated on a daily basis.

Whenever we encountered these challenges, it was comforting to have Randy in the forefront. His physical size alone was intimidating, all six feet and more, and needless to say, the fact that an African-American man was holding such a responsible position of leadership was unexpected to those outside of the church. Little did they know of the kind and sensitive person inside the imposing figure before them.

Randy built a strong support team for the times we faced. Negail Riley, Leonard Miller, and other staff all worked hard to respond creatively to the challenges around us and most importantly to help educate The UMC from within. Programs like the Interreligious Foundation for Community Organization (IFCO), community developers, and others were established then and some still exist to this day. (IFCO has worked for more than thirty years to advance the struggles of oppressed people for justice and self-determination.)

Randy's vision and sensitivity to the concerns of those times kept the National Division on the front line of the encounters. He often led other mainline denominations to join in ecumenical responses to justice needs and changes in prejudicial practices that had been deeply ingrained in our church structures and patterns of operation.

In 1980 when I was elected bishop and assigned to the Philadelphia Area (Eastern Pennsylvania and Puerto Rico annual conferences), I was also assigned as an episcopal member to the General Board of Higher Education and Ministry (GBHEM) for eight years. While I was president of GBHEM, we cooperated with GBGM in one of the greatest missional endeavors in The UMC in decades. We planned and brought into being the Africa University in Zimbabwe. In the beginning of the concept, some members of GBGM felt our educational efforts should be concentrated on strengthening and expanding our many elementary and high schools sponsored by the annual conferences of The UMC in Africa. Randy caught the vision that the time had come for our church to be involved in higher education on the continent of Africa. It was quite evident that even in the U.S., if we had waited to strengthen all of our elementary and high schools before we started colleges and universities, we would be in awful educational shape today. We still have weak pre-college schools in every city, but every year young minds move through them to benefit from higher education in our universities.

Randy and two additional representatives of GBGM have served on the board of Africa University from its inception. Without the support of the members and staff of GBGM, the dream of Africa University would have been much more difficult. The experience of a missional presence in Zimbabwe for ninety years in Old Mutare made a significant difference in all of our negotiations with the government, since we were plowing new ground as the first private university approved by the Zimbabwe Government.

In 1988 I was assigned again to GBGM and served as president of the National Division and vice president of GBGM and then in 1992–1996 as president of the Board. In my second eight years with GBGM, I was constantly impressed with the mature and thoughtful leadership of Randy as general secretary in perhaps the most critical, political time in the life of our UMC.

As leader of the Board with the largest program budget in our church, the politics of the budgets are always focused on the bottom lines. Though much of the GBGM budget is restricted for specific donor-designated and some board-designated usage, the focus of the church is often on the budget as a whole, with little concern for the restricted limitations. The budget is always difficult to interpret across the church. For example, restricted funds must be used only for the purposes the donors direct, and many fund balances must be maintained to enable a quick response for our missionaries in many troubled areas of our world.

The contributors of this book will help to identify some of the multifaceted and complex areas of mission we have served in the twentieth century. All have been directors of the Board at some time during 1980–2002, except for Bishop Pagura. The years of service indicated begin with the year following election to the Board, since quadrennia in The UMC officially begin on January of the year following General Conference and end December 31 the year General Conference is held. Bishop Martinez's full term as president is 2000–2004, although his contribution here covers only 2000–2002.

Bishop F. Herbert Skeete

CHAPTER 1

A Journey of Amazing Grace
Ann Rader Pfisterer (1981–1984)

Two years into my term as president of the National Program Division (1981–1984), one of my daughters and I were talking about the art of conversation at social gatherings. I confessed that my interest, reading, thinking, and planning were focused on the issues and challenges before the General Board of Global Ministries (GBGM) and particularly with the concerns of the National Division. I recall saying to her, "Not everyone wants to hear about the National Division." As though she had been waiting for the right moment, she shot back, "Mother, you're exactly right; not everyone wants to hear about that!"

Captive audiences always responded positively, however, when invitations to speak at local churches afforded the opportunity to tell inspiring and exciting stories about ways United Methodists have worked in partnership with others to offer Christ, relieve misery and change circumstances, develop indigenous leadership, and bring added resources to those who need them.

Now, after more than twenty-five years, I have the opportunity to reflect and write on that amazing journey. It's a gift! I do it gladly but with fair warning that no mention of research accompanied the invitation. My closet of files no longer exists. I have a few letters, articles, etc.; but memories are the chief resource I bring to the task—memories of persons who have responded in countless ways to God's call to be in mission and who have enriched my life in ways I could never repay.

The overwhelming majority of us who have been elected to serve on the general level of our denomination could join a mighty chorus of hallelujahs for the privilege and the challenges of being a director of a program board. Prior to my election, I recall occasionally referring to directors as "they." It was a jolt to realize that "they" became "we" in the decade of the seventies.

Stretched to the limit mentally, spiritually, physically, and emotionally, it was for me a time of discovery, of making difficult decisions, defending positions, working through conflict, and above all remembering that the church is about the God-given task of redeeming the world. There was also the constant, sobering reminder that ignorance and ineptness have severe consequences.

Serving for Two Quadrennia

I was elected to GBGM in 1976 through the processes of United Methodist Women (UMW). *Response* magazine, the Reading Program, and Schools of Christian Mission, in which I participated both as student and teacher, afforded me a Christian mission education that no college or university could match. By 1984, I had thirty-five years of membership in the women's organization. With this election, I realized that I had served or was now serving at every organizational level of both The United Methodist Church (UMC) and UMW.

In 1964, significant changes were made in the structure of mission in the then-Methodist Church. Agreements were carefully and intentionally hammered out to assure that the variety of mission programs formerly administered and supported by Methodist women through the Woman's Division would include the participation of Woman's Division members in policy making. This participation was achieved by the assignment of Woman's Division directors to other parts of the Board. Woman's Division directors went to the site of the Board meeting a couple of days early to complete their agenda prior to the full Board meeting.[1]

For all of us, election meant being away from home. Often meeting dates fell on birthdays, anniversaries, and events in the local church and community. More importantly, it meant becoming an oft-absent homemaker, spouse, and parent. The fallout among families during those eight years I know about was one of the sobering realities of being a director. This was a serious commitment.

Dr. Tracey K. Jones, Jr., general secretary of the Board, greeted us newcomers in 1976 with the story of meeting a Board member after she had completed a twelve-year tenure. He asked her what she was doing with her new-found freedom. Her response was: "The first thing I did was go and have the chair surgically removed!" Serious in his demeanor, this former China missionary and deeply committed leader of our church told us that we could do what we wanted in our "free time," which we could expect between 2:30 and 4:30 A.M. The rest of the time belonged to the Board. We laughed. That is, the new directors laughed. The re-elected directors knew he was at the heart of truth. This was especially true of Women's Division directors.

Focusing on the 1981–1984 Quadrennium

Following my first quadrennium, the telephone rang in our parsonage in Henderson, Kentucky. It was time to reorganize for the new quadrennium. Bishop Frederick Wertz was on the other end of the line. He said, "Ann, I have been asked by the Board Nomination Committee to invite you to be the nominee for a vice president of the General Board of Global Ministries and president of the National Division." I was stunned. Bishops (male) had always chaired the divisions of the Board, with the obvious exception of the Women's Division. Bishops brought the authority of the office (i.e., clout) as they presided in the plenary sessions of the Board. Bishop Wertz was asking me, a woman and layperson, to be the nominee!

New and untested ground was about to be plowed in the National Division. I was not nearly as confident as Bishop Wertz that I was the one to chair the National Division. During the impossibly short period of time I had to consider his request and respond, the urgent question for me was: What do I have to give? Finally, my answers were time, my presence and informed interest, a devotion to Christ, and a commitment to the mission task of the church. With full, loving support from my family, I gathered courage, stepped out on faith and said yes.

On September 11, 1980, the Women's Division presented the following citation:[2]

> To whom it may concern—now and in the future. The Women's Division takes notice and rejoices in the "coming of age" of the administration of its mission work which was merged in 1964.

> We take note of this historic event of yesterday, September 10, 1980, when the Board of Global Ministries for the first time elected a president of World or National Division whose leadership and membership stems from the organization of United Methodist Women.
>
> Ann, your election to this position is a mark of maturation in the development of mission in our denomination. It comes at a moment in world history when through the United Nations attention is at last being focused on the role of women. It comes at the culmination of a century of mission effort by United Methodist Women.

This was truly a "mission initiative," an action within GBGM which gave credence to the commitment long worked towards in the Women's Division for the empowerment of women, of whatever race or culture.

It seemed obvious to me that Dr. Randolph Nugent, head executive of the National Division, would have had to be supportive for my name to go forward as nominee for president. Perhaps the support came from the previous quadrennium. He, with the Reverend Robert Harman, staffed the Research and Development Committee of the Board. As members of that committee, we had tackled some big issues together. I was impressed by the brilliance of Randy's mind, his membership in "think-tanks," access to world church and political leaders, and knowledge of the conditions of the world affecting mission, both denominationally and ecumenically.

The *vision* of our church at work in the world was a continuing committee agenda item. It was here that issues which by their nature shape the mission of the church could be discussed in far greater depth than in the plenary sessions of the Board. In this arena recommendations were hammered out consistent with the vision of being in mission in a changing world. The relevance and the future of the mission task were the driving forces of the Research and Development Committee. Of course, the *Book of Discipline*, which declares the mission mandate of the denomination, was a constant resource. Our task was to assess the needs in the world and the changing styles of doing mission and ministry in compliance with the Disciplinary statements.

I recall that a theologically inclusive committee with regional representation and with both women and men, and a committee that was racially diverse, undertook to study and arrive at a revised mission statement. I was never sure that it got as far as a resolution to General Conference. (This statement was different from the Theology of Mission Statement developed later in the 1980s.) There was, however, great value in the discussions because, for each of us, they refocused our thoughts on *the mission* of God's changing church in God's changing world.

Here also, the Board dealt with the perennial preoccupation of the church—restructure. It is difficult to see this as a mission imperative. It seems far more like a costly waste of time. Again, we spent hours examining the *Discipline* with its fourteen responsibilities for mission. How could these be carried out in different configurations with representation at less financial cost? I have reflected at each subsequent General Conference, with its call for committees to study and to recommend restructuring the general level of the denomination, that if "form follows function," over time, a very similar structure would evolve.

Each quadrennium meant a newly gathered community of faith—a time of discovery. Outstanding leaders of the worldwide church, youth, bishops, able spokespersons, people with new insights, General Conference delegates, theologians, lay people, lifelong missionaries, volunteers in mission, ethnic minorities, people with special interests and professional expertise, people whose first languages were other than English, plodders and planners with a political bent—we were a community of differences. We were a Christian faith community with varied theological perspectives, each one dedicated to faithful service and to personal "causes" inherent in all globally representative bodies. We held one thing in common. Someone had sufficient confidence in each of us to express that confidence in an election process.

Spiritual nurture was a constant agenda item for directors and executive staff members. Someone outside of this amazing community would be surprised to learn of the amount of time spent in worship and study toward a deeper understanding of God's purposes for God's world. We needed better to understand Liberation Theology coming out of South America during the decades of the 1970s and 1980s. The same was true for Black Theology and the Muslim faith. All had and have tremendous implications for the Christian mission task.

We were lifted by experiences of worship led by members and outside speakers, made more articulate by the questions and answers of others, inspired by leaders far more courageous than ourselves, informed by "hands-on" people who experienced challenges and privations we could not even imagine. There was always the premise that you cannot be in mission and ministry without a fundamental respect for an understanding of people—where they are, how they got there, and what they understand their needs to be.

Partnership in mission was the *defining criteria* for developing strategies for mission and ministries. Amid the prevailing criticisms of the "we-they" approach to the "pagans" in the nineteenth century, we sought to affirm the dedication and privations of those who went to the far places for a lifetime. Yet we intentionally moved toward a much more cooperative style of working together. This sounds easy. We looked within ourselves, at one another, and to executive staff persons in a shared experience so we could make informed and worthy decisions. I recall being present at a missionary conference where shared, profound pain and struggle made us deeply aware of our need for prayers of petition for discernment.

Being in Mission—and in Controversy

The National Division was a diverse, driven division. It seemed to me that in the 1970s and early 1980s the policies and practices of this division, along with the Women's Division, were the most scrutinized and criticized of all the units of the general Board. The Good News movement regarded the World Program Division as also problematic. The United Methodist Committee on Relief (UMCOR) has always enjoyed warmer identification and relationships with local churches and annual conferences.

In the late 1970s the Health and Welfare Ministries Division was going through difficult times because of the Pacific Homes law suit. Costs to the denomination in legal fees and settlements ran into the millions of dollars and reverberated into the denominational representative membership of hospital boards and other historically church-related institutions. The financial package to settle the suit was put together from a number of sources. Millions came from GBGM. Redirecting these mission dollars within the Board had a serious impact on the Board's mission initiatives and existing, required program support. Many mission initiatives had to be abandoned or placed on indefinite hold.

I find it incredible that on this very day, as I am reliving these memories and putting them on paper, we have received the Kentucky Conference Monthly paper, *Netnews*, with a 1½-page article entitled, "Pacific Homes saga ends on an up note."[3] The article details the grief and losses during those hard years when a costly, negotiated settlement was finally worked through. But it also shares the good that has flowed from this dreadful experience. In retrospect, we can say: How could we have doubted the outcome when God is in all things working for good? This great affirmation is much clearer today than it was in the agony of discussions with the lawyers, difficult plenary sessions, directors' votes, and countless meetings that siphoned time away from mission concerns.

"Equipping the Mission"

Concerns for the world's women and children have dictated both the initiatives and imperatives of the Women's Division agenda from its beginning. Dedicated mission dollars have given women the right to be heard in the local church, in General Conference, and at all levels in between. Mission is about the wholeness of *all* of God's people.

The position that I occupied for four years made me privy both to the experiences of others and to some interesting ones of my own. It is out of these personal experiences that I would hope to indicate the continuing challenge to empower women and minorities.

Although the staff executive at the head of a division certainly has the right to experience qualms at the prospect of a new working relationship with a woman of the laity at the helm, so does the newly elected president! I was privileged to work with outstanding leaders.

Dr. Nugent is a man with at least four earned degrees—his first as a Crusade Scholar. Multilingual, he has a physical presence that dominates a room, and his mind never stops working. If "keeping the big picture" is as important as we are led to believe, he personifies this. An ordained minister, a deeply spiritual man with a heart for people, he has a passion for the missional task—not just for programs, but also for understandings that shape the task biblically, culturally, socially, and politically. His commitment to travel to the site, meet the people involved, and hammer out understandings in a collegial process is simply his style of being in mission. To those who know him well, he is "Randy."

Rapid change and multiple factors at work in the world demand constant attention. With limited time to read the profusion of relevant books, Randy enlisted the help of the late Dr. J. Edward Carothers, an avid reader and master of digest. Carothers was the head of the National Division prior to Randy's tenure. After his retirement he reviewed significant books for Randy, who circulated the reviews to interested, staff, directors, and friends. Through a wide range of reading, Carothers searched for about twelve books a year he considered of merit. His was a culling process towards reading the most consequential books about global mission. He targeted content to help inform our understanding of the church's mission in the world. He finally retired from this task because of failing eyesight. He has the deep gratitude of many of us who feel far better informed through his dedicated reading and great ability to share. The mantle has been passed, and this valuable service continues. This service is another dimension of "equipping for mission," a phrase all directors know well! "Equipping for mission" means the church provides resources, training, and other forms of preparation for those going into mission as missionaries, professionals, or volunteers.

Dr. Nugent is probably seen and known by the ecumenical and Methodist/United Methodist constituencies as well as local and regional political leaders of the world better than any other person in the life of The UMC today. Constantly reaching out, he is mindful of history, of the debt we owe to those who have sacrificed so much to remain faithful to the mission task. He tells that history often in the hope it will not be lost. For example, he speaks of former missionaries deployed by the Board. They possessed both first-hand knowledge and dedication to the mission task and were great assets to the Board. Following my election in 1976, I became aware that Tracey Jones, Harry Haines (the head executive of UMCOR), and Lewistine McCoy, in the treasurer's office, had been missionaries to China. I'm sure many others on the staff had also been missionaries. The "connection" was invaluable and one that Randy cherished.

Being rather outspoken during my first quadrennium, I recall one of the few pieces of advice I received from Dr. Nugent upon my election. It was a cautionary one! I should understand from the outset that when I spoke, he said, it could or would be understood as speaking for the division or Board and not necessarily as an expression of personal opinion. In the helpful spirit in which it was said, it proved to be a very valuable and face-saving piece of advice, not only in the Board but also in the General Council on Ministries (GCOM).

Serving on GCOM

At the beginning of the 1981 quadrennium, I was elected to represent GBGM in GCOM. Throughout the quadrennium, the updates, informa-

J. Edward Carothers, chief executive of the National Division, Methodist Board of Missions and United Methodist Board of Global Ministries, 1964–1972. *(Photo courtesy of United Methodist Archives and History)*

tion, and explanation of current happenings of the work of the Board to GCOM demanded time and careful attention. This agency is charged with coordinating the work of all the program agencies of the church, which included GBGM.

Prior to the first council meeting, I recall speaking to Betsy Ewing, long-time executive and staff member. She knew the Board and the council's history and responsibilities as few others did. I came away from that conversation with the understanding that this was primarily the general secretaries' arena for reporting and interpreting the work of the various boards and agencies.

Randy, however, saw my election as an opportunity for a joint working relationship. There was one council meeting I remember well. A hot issue in the National Division was on the council agenda. It had long since spilled over into the church. When the presiding bishop either forgot or ignored the prompt that I was to give the report on this item, he introduced Randy. Without a moment's delay, I stepped forward with the impulsive remark that I could understand his confusion since Randy and I looked alike! We could laugh together as we dealt with the most controversial issues.

Empowering Women and Minorities

The empowerment of women and minorities was a hard pill for some to swallow. Randy will remember a prime example as we worked with the Korean Methodist Church in the development of new Korean congregations in the U.S. Perhaps "baffled" best describes the executive secretary of the Korean church when he realized that he, the Methodist bishops of South Korea, seminary professors, and other male leaders in Seoul were to host a small delegation from the National Division that included a woman. In all of his prior dealings, the secretary had dealt with men of whatever rank and title — never with a woman president.

Issues with profound ramifications for the rapidly developing Korean congregations in the U.S. were on the agenda. Would the Korean church establish its own sending agency for clergy of these new congregations, or would the clergy come through the existing National Divison channel? How long would these able young ministers and seminary students stay in the U.S. before returning to South Korea? The possible "brain drain" of their brightest and best was a vital concern.

No condescension, no equivocation, no apologies were ever made for the division president to my knowledge. Randy's consistent attitude was, "She is the president. You talk with her. It makes no difference that the president is a woman." Randy's empowerment and support of women and minorities have been a consistent pattern of his leadership, and more importantly, an affirmation of acceptance at a far deeper level than circumstances or propriety would dictate. I believe it is a faith principle that he continues to employ as he works with both volunteers and staff members in the Board and beyond.

As for the Koreans' acceptance, arriving at the meeting site, I walked into the conference room a few minutes early. Two women rose from their sets and bowed. I was mortified. Soon, I learned that one of the women, Mrs. Oknah Kim Lah, was the president of the World Federation of Methodist Women, and a resident of Seoul. I should have been acknowledging her presence with a bow. She identified herself to me and told me that because of my anticipated presence, the organizers of the conference had invited her and a "Bible woman" to join the delegation. (My understanding was that "Bible women" were trained in understanding the Bible and led study groups, although they were not ordained.) This was the first time she had received recognition in South Korea for her position. They told me that my presence broke down the historic walls that kept women from participating at that level of the church. In a letter dated October 13, 1981, she wrote, "It was a real privilege for me and the Korean church to welcome you to Korea. Your presence must have influenced men to invite women. We hope that you will come back."

Our delegation had been urged to stay over Sunday and participate in church services. I had the time to do that. Walking on the streets of Seoul on a Saturday afternoon, totally alone, not knowing the language, I nevertheless caught a glimpse of the freedom men have experienced for generations. At that moment I was not sure this was a freedom I coveted!

Early Sunday morning a car arrived, and I was escorted by the secretary himself to a thirty-thousand-plus membership church. The opening hymn was announced, and to my amazement it was a Western tune I knew well, as were all of the hymn tunes that morning—remnants of an earlier day in the mission of the church.

I recall vividly that before I left Seoul, the executive secretary of the Korean church had to submit to interrogation by the security police concerning the content and purpose of our meeting. This was a sharp reminder of the scrutiny under which the church was living at the time. Although I certainly knew of the persecution of the church in a number of places in the world, this was my first time actually to witness it up close. It was a sobering experience.

Harder to deal with was the reality that some U.S. bishops had problems with a woman president. One incident had to do with issues concerning one of the mission schools under the aegis of the National Division. I arrived at the area bishop's office before Bishop Ralph Ward, who was serving as interim division head following Dr. Nugent's election to the office of general secretary of the Board. It became very clear that the resident bishop had no intention of discussing his concerns with me. I was relegated to the outer office. He worked at other business until Bishop Ward arrived. When the resident bishop stated that he was now ready for the conference, Bishop Ward said in a matter-of-fact voice, "I don't know why you didn't begin the discussion with Mrs. Pfisterer. She knows as much or more about the situation than I do." A silent "thank you" arose from the depths of my heart. My gratitude was directed not only to Bishop Ward but also to Randy and a supportive staff for the careful briefings and background papers that enabled my informed participation in the task at hand. Empowerment is a community effort!

Eradicating Racism

Racism and what we came to understand as institutional racism were on every agenda of each organized part of the Board during my eight-year tenure. This was at the time the Reverend Woodie White, later elected bishop, led the Commission on Religion and Race. The reports that came to me as a result of the continuing evaluation of the division and the Board demanded changes with the mandate to develop goals, strategies, and timelines to effect the needed changes. Responses had to be returned to the commission for monitoring.

The missional priority of the Ethnic Minority Local Church was a priority for the whole denomination, but the National Division had leadership responsibilities. The division had nurtured the minority caucus groups and sought to empower minority individuals for personnel and program development. Community developers and black community developers had been trained over time. The integrity of the division was at stake in dealing with racism.

The commission looked at executive staff members of units and did not always like what it saw. I recall the stinging criticism of the executive staff of the Office of Finance and Field Service, which was predominantly white, clergy, and male. These persons were being assigned to local churches, many of them ethnic minority, to direct fund-raising campaigns for new church buildings, renovation, indebtedness, operating budgets, and other needs.[4]

Consultants were brought in to help us see ourselves at the deepest levels of attitudes and actions. We began to separate personal racist attitudes and institutional racist practices in our thinking so as to deal with the inherent problems as intentionally as we could. Local churches were dealing with racial issues. Sensitivities were high. The late Thelma Stevens is a person no Women's Division director of that vintage will forget. Christian Social Concerns, which she headed during the turbulent days of the civil rights struggles, formed the core of her being. What a dynamo!

The most tension-fraught race issue of my Board experience unfolded between the National Division and an annual conference. This involved an African-American mayor's conduct, executive staff and field staff actions, and annual conference and its council on ministries leadership. Secular news articles and the church press captured the attention of the constituency. Opinions were formed on less than full and factual information.

This was a terrible issue for the National Division to have to capitulate on. At risk was the integrity of the division in its historic relationship with the Black Caucus, black community developers, leaders of training events — so much that had been a part of the church's historic commitment to racial empowerment and equality. At equal risk was the integrity of the division as it related to annual conferences.

After Dr. Nugent was elected general secretary, the Reverend René Bideaux was elected to follow him as head executive of the National Division. A clergyman, person in mission, respected Board director the prior quadrennium, one with knowledge of the church and its missional task, and one who had a working relationship with the National Division and Board as director of the Hinton Rural Life Center in North Carolina, he was amply qualified for the job.

The ensuing dialogue was fast and furious and would not go away. The area bishop, whose anger was genuine, showed great leadership as he negotiated between the conference council and the division. It is an understatement to say it was tough going. René Bideaux was baptized by fire.

Amid the proliferation of charges and countercharges, it became fairly clear that the assigned staff of the National Division had not kept faith with the negotiated procedures for going into the conference through the conference council on ministries. In a racially charged situation, this issue became the battleground. The overzealous field staff member and her supervisor, who had chosen to ignore proper entry procedures, had to be fired. Staff and directors chose sides. Even as I write this, I can hear others say, "But Ann . . . ."

René and I had worked together in the Research and Development Committee of the Board from 1977 to 1980. I had experienced his Christian spirit and knowledge of the church, and I knew a bit about his personal contacts with persons within conference structures. So much healing had to take place. The Board Committee to Eliminate Institutional Racism took up the cause with a list of demands. I recall that after a sleepless night, I finally got up. My mental wheels had been turning for hours. As rapidly as I could write on a handy scrap of paper, I wrote approximately ten statements which I thought might be of help to the division and Board in the current fray and move us forward with determination and healing. They were well accepted and later appeared in a publication designed to preserve parts of the Board's history.

Emerging/Continuing Issues: Homosexuality

Two high-profile, explosive issues, fueled by articles in the secular press and particularly the *United Methodist Reporter* were not only on the agenda of the National Division but also of deep concern to the Board, GCOM, and the entire church. These issues emerged in the early days of the Good News movement. Criticism of the Board's policies and actions facilitated this movement's growth. I cannot describe the time, energy, soul-searching, research, and pain required of all of us. Randy and I had many theological discussions which provided much context regarding racist and homosexual issues.

The homosexual issue had come to the fore in the Women's Division toward the end of the 1977–1980 quadrennium. An executive staff member, deaconess, and regional secretary informed the division directors that she was a lesbian and wanted to continue in her assignment with her deaconess relationship. The issue galvanized the Women's Division and became a continuing issue for the National Division in the next quadrennium, because the deaconess and home missionary relationships were lodged in the National Division.

In the emotional atmosphere of the plenary sessions in the Women's Division, I came to realize that I had not been elected to the Board to act as a surrogate mother to a young, talented self-confessed lesbian, but to recognize that GBGM in all of its organizational parts is accountable to the General Conference and that changes to the *Discipline* and the Social Principles are properly made within the province of the General Conference, not in the Board or any division of it.

In the meantime, it was the responsibility of the National Division to deal with the issue of the deaconess relationship. Civil rights leaders, young people, and directors of various theological persuasions clashed in the plenary sessions. It was challenging to preside in an explosive atmosphere, mentally to wade through Robert's *Rules of Order* as political and parliamentary tactics were employed by persons who were certainly not novices in any arena — church boards, legislative, or various other political arenas. Demands for explanations of actions and inactions flooded us.

Prior to being elected to the Board, I had chaired the Kentucky Annual Conference Division of Missions and was a conference and jurisdiction officer in UMW. It was no surprise that some local churches and UMW local units reacted to issues in the Board variously—ignoring some and threatening to withdraw from membership and/or withhold financial support. These kinds of grassroots responses add their own dynamic to a discussion. Although the discussion in the National Division was necessary and proper, the issues were dealt with in ways consistent with the *Discipline*.

Continuing the Ethnic Minority Local Church

In addition to the issues, which consumed enormous amounts of his time, René was committed to certain needs he observed in the division, some inherited from the prior quadrennium. For example, consultants were needed for specific jobs when the budget would not allow for the hiring of full-time employees. The missional priority, Ethnic Minority Local Church, required these kinds of special resources from two units of the division: Congregational Development and Parish Ministries. Significant mission initiatives came out of studies and plans of action in these two areas particularly. René saw the value of continuing off-site retreats for spiritual and team growth and for elimination of institutional racism. He sought to encourage teamwork approaches that required clarification of job descriptions, intentional orientation, and retraining of valued employees. All of these initiatives were directed toward greater internal efficiency and more effective support to annual conferences and local churches as they were dealing with the missional priority.

Administering Program in Women's Division Properties

Another targeted area was the working relationship with the Women's Division. At that point I had more than thirty-one years of membership in UMW. As previously stated, my vision and understanding of missions had been nurtured through that channel. The National Division, under the 1964 restructuring of the Board, was given the administration of programs within Women's Division–owned properties. Through cooperative efforts that continued into the next quadrennium, we were brought to new beginnings. Initiatives had come from both divisions and from administrative/program directors in the field. As partners, we undertook to move forward.

Interpreting Mission to the Local Church

Interpreting mission to the local church has always been a challenge. The Education and Cultivation Division continued to address this task. Leaders of jurisdictional events offered suggestions and resources to annual conferences and local churches to inform and interest local congregations to get more intentionally involved in mission. I know firsthand the various ways we sought to interest local pastors. This area of communication has been difficult at best and totally frustrating most of the time. Many members of local churches have no knowledge of the extraordinary, creative, exciting ministries available for their personal and financial involvement.

In the 1981–1984 quadrennium we had a national mission event in the western part of our country. This has since been followed by "global gatherings" that have been inspiring and informative to the world Methodist community. The sad thing is I have sat in worshiping congregations and heard clergy exalt missions and ministries outside of The UMC. To my knowledge and experience, our church is doing a better job in the same areas of concern, and they don't know it! The grassroots for mission initiatives is limitless. In many of those areas, the Board stands ready with helpful resources which are being developed and improved all the time. For example, "Church and Community Profile," developed by the Research Office, provides a wealth of data—at a minimal cost to every local church in the denomination. This is an indispensable tool for the visioning process in which many churches are engaged.[5]

Supporting Volunteers in Mission

A successful mission initiative which began in the Southeastern Jurisdiction and later moved into the National Division structure, Volunteers in Mission (VIM) is a ministry that has brought excitement and spiritual renewal to many individuals and congregations. VIM consists of people with medical knowledge, construction skills, bilingual abilities, homemaking experience, music experience, preaching ability, Bible study skills, well-digging training, and many other needed resources and abilities. They have formed teams and gone at their own expense to work under the supervision of receiving congregations in Central and South America, the Philippines, and many other places. They build schools and churches, minister to health and spiritual needs, and do many other tasks. Working as partners in mission adds an undeniable satisfaction to being in mission as well as adding some frustrations. Partnership is a missional necessity.

I recall an intern program, initiated during my tenure on the Board, for college graduates with study in the U.S.; then a placement in a mission position for a certain number of months, many times abroad; followed by a third period of time back in the U.S. Responses from this program were gathered by the World and National divisions. At that time, college graduates faced bleak prospects for getting into jobs in their chosen fields. This was an excellent opportunity for them to see parts of the U.S. and the world, and an opportunity to move from college into the workforce. Outstanding young women and men experienced the church at work in their areas of specialized training. Blessings rebounded to the Board and certainly to the church. The first group in the program wrote an anthology of experiences. It was published and placed in our hands. At least one outstanding young woman who edited the book was subsequently employed by the Board.

Establishing the Southwest Border Consultation

By 1980, initiatives in the Southwest had been fostered over several quadrennia. The National Division had financed a video that provided stark revelations of need on both sides of the U.S.-Mexico border, from Brownsville, Texas, and its sister city of Matamoros, Mexico, to San Diego and Tijuana, Mexico. During my tenure there was no question about the validity of continuing these joint efforts around border issues. With equal representation from both the U.S. and Mexico, this group met regularly to try to make a difference. A number of initiatives were implemented, including the expression of concern about working conditions in the *maquiladoras*, the "twin factories" in Mexico, human rights, health, and poverty.

Continuing Native American Concerns

If I had a single cause while I was president, it was the concerns of Native Americans. I recall vividly that my husband and I drove to Antler, Oklahoma, to the site of the annual Oklahoma Indian Missionary Conference.

At that time the tabernacle was an open-air structure. Abundant rain fell during the conference, making for unpleasant conditions. The families came to camp on site for the meeting. The host tribe, on a rotating basis, had saved a portion of its harvests to feed the conference. Meat was brought in on hoof, slaughtered, and prepared.

The contrasts—even with the other two missionary conferences, Alaska and Red Bird—were stark. I heard the concerns: no money for church roofs or other needed repairs, the need for ministerial training, and the need for higher salaries, to name only a few. I know there have been changes. The area bishop brought creative, strong leadership during my tenure.

My husband, Fred, and I were there from the opening prayer through the benediction, a presence many Native Americans appreciated. I recorded earlier that my acceptance of the office of president was based on a commitment of time. Being there was a heart-warming and convicting experience for both of us. The highlight of my entire eight years of general Board service culminated in the final night session under the stars as each tribal chief came to the front to lead his tribe in a time of singing. We experienced in that place with those amazing people a Pentecost beyond description, as the evening ended with ten tribes, each in its own language, and a very few of us in English, singing together, "Amazing grace, how sweet the sound . . . ."

My journey was one of amazing grace. My life has been blessed. I am truly grateful.

CHAPTER 2

The Origin and Creation of a Theology of Mission Statement
Betty S. Gordon (1981–1988)

𝒯RAVELING FOR THE church is probably not as wonderful as most people think. It is true one sees various places in the U.S. and the world, but what many people do not realize is that most of the time is taken up in meetings and work. That means what you mostly see is the inside of a hotel meeting room. Traveling can sometimes be hazardous to your health, especially if you must go to remote areas without the comforts of civilization. And then there are the unknowns of travel.

I experienced this when I traveled to Switzerland for one of the global consultations held by the General Board of Global Ministries (GBGM) when I was a director. I had to arrive a day early because of my responsibilities, and I was traveling alone. After arriving in Zurich I took a train and then a bus to the small town of Hasliberg-Reuti high in the Swiss Alps and in the German-speaking part of the country. The bus driver let me off at the end of the road in the rain. When I arrived at the front desk, the hotel staff told me they had no room for me. I sat down and thought, "Lord, you brought me to this place, now what am I going to do?"

We have all heard of angels of mercy. One showed up at that moment in the form of Dr. Randolph Nugent, the general secretary of the Board. I was overjoyed to see him, and he listened to my problem. Randy, which is what we learned to call him, went to the front desk and said, "Give this woman my room." It was a very nice room, and Randy found other accommodations. But after this act of mercy on his part, I told him, "You have a long list of items on the good side of the column." My prayer had been answered.

This trip and the important Board initiative I want to share with you was summarized on October 28, 1986, in a United Methodist Communications press release, written by Frances Smith. It stated, "A new theology of mission, hammered out over three years with input from Methodists on five continents, ecumenical Christians and U.S. conservative-evangelicals, was approved by 179 directors of the United Methodist Board of Global Ministries.

"It proclaims unabashedly that the mission is God's" and "Christians are called to be partners in mission with God."

"Pointing out signs of God's mission, the new theological statement says God's authority *sends* the church into mission, God's power *sustains* the church in mission and God's revelation in Jesus Christ *defines* the church in mission. The church is to be an indicator of God's presence in the world and a reminder of God's image in Christ."

Revealing the Story Behind the Release

Now let me tell the story of how this important statement came to be written.

When Randolph Nugent was elected general secretary of GBGM in 1981, he issued a call to review the Board's theological statements related to mission. He reminded the Administrative Committee that changes were taking place in mission and the manner by which the Board was viewed by the church and the Board itself. He also said there was an understanding that the Board had not looked at itself recently in terms of a theological position relating to mission and that theological foundations were essential for program planning.

The Administrative Committee responded by directing the Research and Development Committee to develop a theology of mission statement that would encompass the entire biblical perspective and the manner by which all of the Board units do their work. A proposal to the Board for a task force to prepare a theological statement of mission for the General Board of Global Ministries was made as follows:

> A continuing and more rapidly changing world demands a constant attention to needed changes in theological thinking. Theology which is relevant to the existing human condition while being faithful to our tradition can be a significant motivating factor for action in the world

by the Church and its people. Theology is one of the principal reasons for the uniting and dividing of the Church.

A current statement of the theology of mission would be valuable to the Church as it ministers to the world. In addition, the statement would be useful in the framing of program and educating the world on the theological basis of the Board's work.[1]

Naming a Task Force

The newly organized Board in October 1984 named a task force to develop a statement.[2] The Reverend C. Rex Bivens, Nebraska, served as chair. The direction to the task force was to develop a statement "that is faithful to the Biblical witness and Wesleyan tradition and responsive to God's action in the present global context." Further direction was to maintain a relationship with the entire Board, with outreach to the entire church, and to culminate the effort with an event when the Board would present its theological perspective. The time set for this event was spring of 1987 in conjunction with the Board meeting. All work of the task force was to be directed to that date. Prior to the event it was hoped consultations would be held within the Christian community that would reflect the global dimensions of the church in Asia, Africa, Europe, and Latin America as well as the United States.

At the initial meeting, the task force was formed into two teams:

A consultation team would define the purpose of the consultations, develop the design and the process, and identify the constituencies to be reached during the consultation. This team would determine how the consultations would be recorded and in what form they would be preserved.

A drafting team would study and review the data from the consultations, create a process of listening and learning with persons involved, and provide recordings of plenary presentations and small group work. Also, the team would have the responsibility of producing a final draft as the "Theology of Mission Statement."

It was understood that recognition of the general perspective of the Board's mission was important. Consultations were planned to be held, one each in Asia, Africa, Europe, Latin America, and the Caribbean, and four in North America.

Setting up Global Consultations

The consultations were to examine the uniqueness of the context in which the gospel is proclaimed. In addition, they would gather data toward the development of the statement of theology of mission today. The data gathered would be related to the culture, religion, issues, suffering of people, and their aspirations. Data would also be sought concerning ecumenical relationships and the vision of mission for the future.

The consultation team presented the following design for the consultations, and it was accepted by the total task force:

Purpose: "To provide opportunities for listening and dialogue among church colleagues in a variety of mission settings from which the GBGM can draw learnings for the development of a current statement on the Theology of Mission that is faithful to the Biblical witness and the Wesleyan tradition and is responsive to God's action in the present global context."

Locations: Harare, Zimbabwe
Zurich, Switzerland
Singapore
Omaha, Nebraska
San Jose, Costa Rica
Pittsburgh, Pennsylvania
Memphis, Tennessee
Kingston, Jamaica
San Francisco, California

Dates: From August 1985 through March 1986

Participants: The bishop, president of United Methodist Women, chair of conference board of global ministries, and council director of each conference were asked to meet and submit names of twenty persons in a variety of categories that reflected the annual conference. The task force selected persons to achieve potential balance in participation at each event. Invitations to attend the consultations were sent under the signature of the general secretary.

One of the consultations for the Theology of Mission Statement that the General Board of Global Ministries developed was held in Pittsburgh, Penn., in January 1986. *(Photo from General Board of Global Ministries photo library. Photo by Linda Elmiger)*

The drafting team prepared and presented a document as a "listening agenda."

Drafting team members were asked to be active listeners and reporters of key content and expressions of theologies in local and regional settings. The Reverend James R. McGraw was selected as the writer of the theology of mission statement.[3]

Holding the Consultations

The directors divided responsibility for participation in the various consultations. I myself took part in consultations held in Memphis, Pittsburgh, Omaha, Switzerland, and Costa Rica. After the incident described in the introduction to this paper, the consultation in Switzerland was held, and representatives from all over Europe were there, but the consultation was held in English. At one time I was privileged to be paired with the Reverend Bodo Schwabe from Germany. He also served as a director of GBGM and in the German Methodist Church (Central Conference in the Federal Republic of Germany and West Berlin) had a position approximating that of Dr. Nugent. We discovered we had some differences, but our commitment to mission was something we had in common.

The consultation in Costa Rica was quite different, of course, because then we were in a tropical climate. Furthermore we were meeting at a time when civil wars were raging in Nicaragua and El Salvador. Representatives from the Latin American countries as well as Central America were there, and the consultation was held in Spanish, with translators for those of us who spoke another language.

Our hosts were very courteous and each night at the end of the meeting they arranged music, dancing, or some other form of entertainment. When we had communion, the service was open and less formal than ours in the U.S. Since I was assigned to work with the Latin America/Caribbean area of the World Program Division, which Nora Boots headed, I was glad to be working with Nora and that Nora was there.

One of the beneficial aspects of the consultations was that a local committee was responsible for arrangements. Having local committees meant that the consultations were not strictly the Board's and belonged to those in the city and region where we met. I remember the one in Memphis, where part of the meeting was held at First UMC downtown. The local committee had arranged for the Jarvis Brothers, a gospel quartet from Orangeburg, South Carolina, to sing. They impressed us with their renditions of "Dry Bones," "Moses Smote the Water," and "Jacob's Ladder."

Having a group from South Carolina pleased me because that is my native state. Many who know me think that my accent is from West Virginia, where I now live, but it is actually a South Carolina accent. Sometimes people wonder how well those of us with such an accent communicate, especially with those from other countries who may speak English but not exactly our kind of English. My answer is that my accent is a real "plus." It means that each of us in a conversation is forced to explain what we mean about particular words and terms. We usually are friends after going through this exercise.

Planning a Mission Convocation

In February 1985 the task force met with the Mission Convocation Committee of the Board. The Mission Convocation Committee had been created to consider a large event that would enable the Board to address critical mission issues outside the context of religious politics. Such an event, it was thought, would also serve to rally the faithful and develop a greater sense of community among the many involved in mission in The United Methodist Church.[4] Dr. Nugent noted that both the task force and the committee were generated from the Research and Development Committee. He said the convocation would be expected to be the launching pad for the theology of mission statement. The two groups were to work closely as one generated the idea and the other propelled it. Close collaboration, consultation, and communication between the two groups would be necessary. During the discussion there was better understanding regarding programming and the role of participants in the regional consultations and the convocation.

It was agreed by both groups that the theme for the convocation would be "Celebrating God's Mission: A Global Gathering," and the dates would be March 12–15, 1987. The Convocation Committee had been involved in a sophisticated process to determine the location of a suitable site. Louisville, Kentucky, was the site selected.

From the beginning Dr. Nugent strongly stressed it was imperative that the total churches' voices be heard and recognized in the final theology of mission statement. In response to his concern and direction, United Methodist caucuses, agency representatives, seminaries, and others were invited to have an opportunity to contribute to the statement. A hearing was held on April 12, 1986, in New York.

We met in the former Penta Hotel, just across from the entrance to Penn Station. Participants were given an opportunity to present and elaborate on their responses. The following groups accepted the invitation by attending either the hearing and/or submitting responses: MARCHA (Metodistas Associados Representando la Causa de Hispano-Americanos); Garrett-Evangelical Theological Seminary; Drew University Theological School; Mission Society for United Methodists; National Federation for Asian American United Methodists; Affirmation; Good News; and the Methodist Federation for Social Action. The written and oral contributions were reviewed and incorporated into the data.

Including Themes and Issues from Consultations

The drafting team reviewed data from the consultations, the hearing, and the "listening agenda" reports completed by team members and other delegated persons. Identification and listing of key themes, issues, responses, and concerns to be reviewed for the statement included many expressions from the consultations, such as:

> Church and state issues addressed in context of that region (Africa, Asia);
> Contextualization of theology (Africa);
> Dominance of power of the U.S. church (Africa/Asia/Latin America/Caribbean);
> God as creator (Nebraska);
> Economic justice in the church (Latin America);
> Tradition as a major source for/of theology (Africa);
> Role of an evangelist (Africa);
> Missionary's awareness that people are already religious (Africa);
> Evaluation of "sending" missionaries (Europe);
> Retention of "the whole world is my parish" appeal (Europe);
> Faith and understanding of God (Latin America/Caribbean);
> Mission as commitment (Latin America/Caribbean);
> Singing "our" songs, not just changed words of "your" songs (Africa, Caribbean);
> Signs of the covenant (Tennessee);
> Communities of the new covenant equal the church (Pennsylvania);
> Grace! (Africa);
> Saving grace of Christ (California);
> Mission as witness and challenge (California);
> Global community? (Tennessee, Pennsylvania, California);
> Ministries of John Wesley, Francis Asbury, Phillip Otterbein, Martin Boehm, and Jacob Albright (Pennsylvania);
> Evangelization and solidarity as synonymous (Latin America);
> Coconut theology (using the life-cycle of the coconut to communicate christological understanding [Latin America]).

Many more issues were discussed or mentioned. One issue, however, continually surfaced with a particular prominence. That issue was *the safeguarding of the centrality of Jesus Christ in the doctrine of salvation.* The task force agreed biblical and theological expertise to address the issue was needed. Dr. Cain Felder, associate professor of New Testament language and literature at Howard University Divinity School and a United Methodist clergy, was asked to be a consultant. He met with the drafting team and full Theology of Mission Task Force. Dr. Felder prefaced his answers to questions from the drafting team by saying that ancient communities of faith raised ultimate questions in trying to understand the significance of God's redemptive activity in history. These questions, he said, comprise a rich diversity of proclamation and yet we have to understand this diversity in relation to the central *kerygma*, the core of the proclamation, that is also present.

Dr. Felder continued: In the Old Testament there is a double tradition at work. The particularist strand comes from Israel's self-understanding as God's unique people. The universalist strand comes from the prophetic witness that all nations will come to Zion. Neither strand, however, constituted a mandate to "go into all the world" to make God's activity known irrespective of race, ethnicity, and geography. It is left to us to see Christ as the center of time, Christ as a profound new dispensation of God's redemptive activity, so that something new may happen.

Although for Paul, Christ's work is seen as the activity of God, we need to recognize that Paul's theology is more centered on God than on Christ. By emphasizing God we can appreciate the unity of the Bible. We have to deal with the problem of continuity and discontinuity between the Old Testament and the New Testament. The Gospel of Matthew was perfect for this, which is why it was made the first book in the New Testament. We can see this when Matthew uses a genealogy as part of Jesus' Jewish credentials but then mentions Tamar, Rahab, and Bathsheba—women who make up a creative divine discontinuity. The commission at the end of the gospel to "go into all the world" is then something new that has happened and that becomes a mandate for the church.

Dr. Felder also reviewed some passages from the New Testament that emphasize particularity, the way that Christ is the seemingly single way to salvation. He said these texts must be read in the context of the fourfold criteria of Scripture, tradition, experience, and reason. He said, however, it is impossible for any Christian ever to deny that Jesus Christ is Lord in some universal sense. He then responded to specific questions from the team (the answers to the questions are paraphrases of Dr. Felder's comment):

> 1. Do persons in other religious traditions which affirm Jesus Christ as Lord experience salvation?
>
> Dr. Felder said that the mission statement needs to begin with the sovereignty of God in answering this question. The sovereignty of God is the first step to understanding the nature of salvation in the Judeo-Christian tradition. It is in God's own capacity to show forth mercy and compassion and ultimately the centrality of the law of love.
>
> What God has done in Jesus Christ is central in the Christian

proclamation. But this action of God does not mean that salvation is guaranteed. It simply means believers are transported into this arena. We still have to deal with the Wesleyan understanding of sanctification: How do we nurture the life in the Spirit? In the sense that God can manifest Himself in diverse traditions, the answer to the question is yes. But for the Christian, in a confessional sense, the answer is no. To affirm Jesus as Lord is more than a rhetorical obsession, but it is still a formal sign of acceptance of the grace and the possibility of final salvation. We have to be open to the possibility that those who are utterly serious about their own (non-Christian) traditions and live a pious, seeking life are those whom John speaks of in 10:16 as "other sheep not of this fold."

2. Can Christian faith or evangelism take place in forms other than seeking converts or proselytizing?

Basically Dr. Felder's answer to the question is yes. He pointed to New Testament texts where Paul seems to assume that we have a world in common with unbelievers. We have to see the mandate for mission in a global sense as a mandate that is refracted in terms of diverse forms of mission. There is a difference between those alienated from all religion and those like Jews who are religious. The mandate for mission seems particularly applicable to the former.

3. Does the work of Christ achieve salvation for all time, people, and circumstances?

The gospel shows the way to the fullness of life, the abundant life, and this is part of the universal mandate for mission. We might distill the message of the Book of Hebrews into the statement, "Christ is enough." We Christians are under an obligation to show in our lives how Christ is enough. Because Christ is enough in the human situation, we may see our mandate for mission as utterly legitimate, and it should therefore be taken with a new level of enthusiasm for the world.

Following Dr. Felder's response to the questions, the task force members had the opportunity to ask additional questions and discuss concerns. The dialogue was rich with information and insight for the final draft of the statement.

Approving the Mission Statement

A plan was developed to determine what data would be presented in a progress report to the Board. In preparation for the spring meeting a "preliminary draft outline" was shared with the directors and staff to provide a sense of direction of the task force. Major themes were identified, such as:

"Joining God in Mission;
Signs of God's Mission;
Biblical Witness;
Challenges in God's Mission;
Mission for a New Age."

A draft of the statement and a summary were mailed to directors and staff prior to the fall 1986 meeting of the Board. The statement was to be used in defining and planning program strategies. The summary would become the content for a brochure and other publications about the program of the Board. The directors were informed that another document of a longer narrative for study and reflection was still in process and would be a continued assignment for the task force.

At the fall 1986 Board meeting, time was given in the first plenary for the directors and staff to have another opportunity for discussion. The request to the directors and staff in table groups was to respond to the following:

1. Points in the Statement I wish to affirm;
2. Points in the Statement which require clarification;
3. Suggestions for revision.

After the plenary, the task force reviewed and edited responses and suggestions for improving the document. In a second plenary, the task force presented revisions with suggested improvements to the document. In a final plenary, the amended document was presented for final approval.

As the task force made the recommendation for approval of the "Theology of Mission Statement: Partnership in God's Mission," Bishop James Ault, president, read from the statement: "God's Call to mission can be discerned in the signs and challenges of our time. God's prodding presence of the Holy Spirit moves us into personal and corporate confessions, repentance, deepened faith and evangelical witness." He continued, "The church is being swept by the Spirit into a new mission age. We may not yet know where or how the Spirit will lead, but we look forward with faith and hope to a new Pentecostal moment in mission."

The task force had completed the directions of the Board "to develop a statement that is faithful to the Biblical witness and Wesleyan tradition and responsive to God's action in the present global context."

The "Theology of Mission Statement: Partnership in God's Mission" was adopted by the General Board of Global Ministries, October 24, 1986.

In a letter to all who participated in the consultations, Dr. Nugent wrote, "This statement becomes a position paper of the Board for guiding and interpreting its future program directions. It is an articulation of the theology which undergirds the contemporary patterns of fulfilling the historic functions of outreach mission assigned to the Board. It is not intended to be a Disciplinary statement for the general church."

Holding the First Global Gathering

This narrative of the story behind the release continued in the presentation to the total church at the first global gathering, held in Louisville, Kentucky, in March 1987. The statement was presented in a variety of ways with emphasis on the major themes.

The first plenary of the gathering was focused on "Challenges in God's Mission." Archbishop Desmond Tutu of South Africa offered the proclamation at a service of Word and Table. Celebrants were Bishop Onema Fama of then-Zaire (now Democratic Republic of the Congo), Bishop Isaías Gutiérrez of Chile, and the Reverend Sandra Hoke from Illinois. Music presented included a medley of South African songs, African-American drums, and the Rajah Percussion Ensemble and Instrumentalists from the Louisville Symphony.

The theme, "Joining God in Mission Today," was highlighted by a panel that quoted parts of the theology of mission statement, such as: "Because God is present in Christ in every human setting throughout the world, mission partnership must include witness in all cultures, traditions, political arrangements, economic structures and languages. Because God's mission is the work of the Holy Spirit, partners in God's mission must be open and receptive to the manifold manifestations of the Spirit across the face of the earth."

Another panel highlighted other parts of the statement: "Joining God's mission requires mutual sharing and exchange of witness and resources among mission partners. True mission partnership is rooted in mutual love, trust, compassion, sharing, support and respect."

The theme, "Signs of God's Mission Today," was expressed in a service of baptism reaffirmation. Rex Bevins, the chair of the task force, gave the proclamation, and as vice chair, I read from the statement: "The church in mission is a sign of God's presence in the world. By the authority of God and the power of the Holy Spirit, the church joins God's mission to reclaim, restore and redeem the life of all creation to its God-intended design, confessing by word and deed. The United Methodist tradition is a history of participation in God's mission.

"In consultations from Singapore to Switzerland, Zimbabwe to Costa Rica, Jamaica to the United States, we have heard testimony that mission is God's mission, and we are partners in mission with God." The litany taken from the statement was read by members of the Theology of Mission Task Force.

Reaffirmation of baptismal vows was led by Dr. Nugent. Global participants brought offerings of water from their homes all over the world and poured the water into a baptismal font. In return participants filled their jars from the baptismal font while all sang "Springs of Water."

"Mission for a New Age" was the theme of a service of commissioning and recognition. Dr. Nugent presented the sending-forth litany: "The church is being swept by the Spirit into a new mission age. We may not yet know where or how the Spirit will lead, but we look forward with faith and hope to a new Pentecostal moment in mission."

The response of the people was: "Help us to be partners with God in mission!"

The first global gathering, with more than 4,200 in attendance, ended, but the common biblical foundation and ecclesiastical tradition had yielded expressions of faith that reflect varied histories, cultures, and perceptions of the church's response concerning mission in a changing and dynamic global setting.

Giving Meaning to "Mission Partners"

The experience of serving with the theology of mission task force and chairing the drafting team influenced my life in unlimited ways. Many new terms surfaced during the process. One of those was *"Partnership in*

God's mission," and for me that means "as mission partners we strive earnestly to understand one another, to trust and support one another, to depend on one another and to uphold one another through a faith active in love that enables us to be open and receptive to a new mission future." Hearing theology from the global church gives emphasis that "the church is being swept by the Spirit into a new mission age."

As stated in the opening press release, "Pointing out signs of God's mission, the new theological statement says God's authority *sends* the church into mission, God's power *sustains* the church in mission and God's revelation in Jesus Christ *defines* the church in mission. The church is to be an indicator of God's presence in the world and a reminder of God's image in Christ."

Our theology of mission remains a testimony until it is lived. Only then will it be a statement. Amen!

Randolph Nugent, as general secretary and as a member of the task force, continually gave support, encouragement, and cooperation as the task force developed and fulfilled the responsibilities given by the Board. Without his insight the statement may not have been a reality. Developing this statement was a priority for Dr. Nugent and he stressed it was imperative that the total churches' voices be heard and recognized in the final statement. The church listened, heard, and we learned together. It has been my privilege to serve with my friend, Dr. Nugent, on this task force, as a director of the Women's Division and GBGM, as consultant, and as interim staff serving on the cabinet.[5]

CHAPTER 3

A Servant People to God's Creation
Woodrow Hearn (1989–1992)

*T*HE GENERAL BOARD of Global Ministries (GBGM) as the outreach arm of The United Methodist Church (UMC) relates to several thousand mission activities in 160 countries.

The *Book of Discipline* of The UMC mandates the responsibilities for the general Board and among them is this one: "To discern those places where the gospel has not been heard or heeded and to witness to its meaning throughout the world, inviting all persons to newness of life in Jesus Christ through a program of global ministries."

During the 1989–1992 quadrennium, the Board sought to fill this mandate and its other assigned responsibilities through a wide variety of ministries in many places in the world.

I have become convinced that the mind of no one person can contain knowledge of all the things United Methodist people do in the spirit of Jesus Christ through GBGM. This is the story of some activities of the Board during the quadrennium.

Launching the Russia Initiative

A major new initiative that will have lasting effect in the decades ahead was the establishment of the initiative to Russia. In January 1991, Dr. Randolph Nugent, general secretary, and I, as president of GBGM, went to Moscow excited about the possibilities which might open, though we were not able to predict what might be the outcome of the visit. What has happened in a decade after that visit would have seemed an impossible dream to us in 1991.

Why were we going to Moscow? Our visit was the result of a conversation a United Methodist woman had in Washington, D.C., with representatives of the Soviet Peace Fund. These Soviet people indicated that the Soviet Government would be receptive to conversations with The UMC about ways that our church could work with the Soviet people.

In the dim light of a Moscow winter day, the capital city of the USSR looked the way one would imagine it should look. The historic pastel buildings and tall towers of the Kremlin, historic reminders of the long Russian history, were all lightly dusted with snow.

During the next week we negotiated with several agencies. First was the Russian Orthodox Church, where we were received in one of the old monasteries located close to the center of Moscow that had recently been given back to the church for its use. Renovation work was under way to make it ready to be the headquarters of the patriarch.

The reception we received was very cordial and appreciative. We were there at a time of great transition for the Russian Orthodox Church in what was to be the last months of the existence of the Soviet Union. Many church buildings had been taken from the church after the Communist revolution of 1918. These church properties were used for many purposes, such as schools, manufacturing plants, and warehouses. The Russian Orthodox Church at the time of our visit was receiving five churches a day restored to church control and use.

The large number of church buildings being placed again in the church's hands had created for the Russian Orthodox Church a need for more priests and also for literature. The literature had been destroyed during the Communist period, so church representatives talked to us about ways that we could share with them the United Methodist experience of training clergy and publishing church literature. The Russian Orthodox Church and patriarch at this meeting were very cordial and receptive, indicating that they would welcome The UMC to the Union of Soviet Socialist Republics and give us help in re-establishing our church there. Later this view seemed not to be supported by some who were around the patriarch and who held the view that the Russian Orthodox Church had been the church of that geographic area for a thousand years and others who came there were moving into their territory. To this day, the patriarch's regard for the General Board of Global Ministries and appreciation for Dr. Nugent has remained strong. The general secretary of the Board proved to be a perfect contact person for establishing that relationship.

The excitement created among some of the people by the opening of the church buildings that had been closed or given to secular use is illustrated by a young woman whom we met in Zagorsk. Following a visit to the historic seminary and monastery at Zagorsk, arranged by the partiarch, a lunch had been scheduled to enable us to visit with some of the leaders. One of the translators following the lunch asked if Dr. Nugent and I would come to visit her church before we returned to Moscow. Following her directions our driver turned up a narrow snow-covered road on the edge of the town. On the top of the hill surrounded by a few leafless trees we saw a church building with the onion domes on the roof, trademark of the Russian Orthodox churches. Inside, a worship center with icons had been established in one corner of the nave.

The building had been given back to the Russian Orthodox Church about six months before this visit. Standing in front of the temporary altar, the woman said that there had been several weddings here since the church was returned for religious use. Then she added a sentence that I thought revealed the reason why she was so anxious to have us see the church: "My wedding was the first one held here after the building was returned to the church."

While we were inside the building, five men arrived from town and began breaking up one of the several large brick ovens located on the floor of the nave. The church had been used as a bakery during the years that the building had been taken from the church. Now the space was to be converted back to its original purpose. These five men with chisels and malls were breaking apart the bricks of the former bread ovens to make space once again available for worship. These five men, I realized, were the Soviet equivalent of Volunteers in Mission.

Evidence of the process of religion returning to a place of recognition in the society was illustrated by two incidents that happened while we were in Moscow.

First there was the opening of the Moscow Stock Exchange. The celebration was held in a grand hall illuminated by massive chandeliers, with the walls lined with serving tables heaped with cold hors d'oeuvres for which the Russians are noted, including many dishes filled with several varieties of caviar—more caviar than I ever imagined existed. Beyond the surprise that we were witnessing the opening of a stock exchange, a tool of the capitalistic system, was the additional unexpected appearance of a bishop of the Orthodox Church, who was called upon in the inaugural ceremony to give a prayer of blessing. Obviously a new way of thinking about religion was emerging in what had been the Communist stronghold when a bishop was asked to bless the stock exchange.

A second evidence of this same new reality came while we were visiting an Orthodox church in central Moscow. It was described to us as the capital city's most active and largest church that had continued to be open during all of the revolution years. The priest there wanted us to see some social service work of the parish. We began our visit, however, in the sanctuary of the church building. It was early evening and many people were coming and going, some standing in front of the central altar where a priest was officiating at a service. Others were arranging and decorating the building for the observance of a feast day. While standing in the central aisle near the entrance of the church, we were approached by a camera crew and reporter from Moscow TV requesting an interview with the bishop from America. I took this as another sign of a new openness and interest in religion.

Negotiation with the Soviet Government was an exciting, interesting, and intriguing experience. We met with the heads of two government departments on successive mornings in a government building near the Kremlin. Dr. Nugent and I went with our translator, a young man who spoke English well and at the time was continuing to study in advance language school learning Portuguese. His father was an official in the government in an office that related the central government to the republics in the union—in his case, Estonia. His mother was not employed, which the translator said was fortunate because it allowed her time to stand in line at the shops to buy items of food and clothing needed for the family. I asked him what he thought about the changes that obviously were taking place all around. He said life in some ways was more difficult. Prices were higher and goods were more difficult to find, but the advantage, he explained with a twinkle in his eye, was the way that now he could talk to me openly like this without fear of someone standing behind him listening and reporting what he said.

In the conference room each day, the arrangements were always the same. Dr. Nugent and I sat on one side of the massive conference table with our translator. The head of the government department and his deputy with their translator sat on the other side of the table. Then there was always another person who sat at the end of the table to whom we were not introduced, nor did he ever speak. We assumed that this was the representative of the KGB, the Russian secret police.

Each of the two mornings with the government officials started the same. The head of the department would begin with his greeting and welcoming statement. This was followed by the statement that there were no needs that could not be met by the Soviet Government for the Soviet people. After several minutes of this description of there not being any needs, the department head each day got to what I would call the "but" clause. Here the official would say that it would be good if we could help with some medicines and high-vitamin content food, especially for children and the elderly. Our response was that we were certain that The UMC would want to respond in a helpful way.

The first day the department head replied that when the medicines or food were sent that the government would distribute them. This made me a little uneasy so I responded by saying that whenever our church gives humanitarian aid, the church representatives are involved in its distribution also. The next day, we met with a second department. After the discussion had gone the same as the morning before — denial of any need, then the "but" clause and the identification of medicines, medical equipment, and high-vitamin content foods as areas of help needed — the department head made the same proposal that they would do the distribution. I made the same statement I had made the day before that representatives of our church would want to be connected with the distribution. At once the official responded in a way that led me to believe that he had conferred with the other department head overnight. This could be arranged, he said, and twelve departments of the Soviet Government if needed would be placed at our disposal to help with the distribution. His list of twelve departments that could help included the army, if strong bodies were needed, and the air force, if transportation were required. Number nine on the list was the KGB, but what function they might have was not specified.

Following this visit The UMC did respond by sending several hundred thousand dollars of medical supplies and equipment as well as food items. A United Methodist pastor from Poland was recruited to oversee the warehouse secured in Moscow for a distribution terminal, and the Russian Orthodox Church played a significant role in determining where the supplies should be distributed. The Louisiana Annual Conference took a special interest in gathering supplies, and a Soviet transport of a type reputed to be the largest in the world flew to Barksdale Air Force Base in Bossier City, Louisiana, to be filled with medicines, medical equipment, and food supplies for the Soviet people.

The faces of this man and child in Moscow in 1992 reflect some of the difficulties the people of Russia faced in the immediate aftermath of the dissolution of the Soviet Union. *(Photo by Richard Lord)*

One of the needs to which United Methodists responded was for medical equipment and medicines. This need was illustrated for us by a visit to the Central Children's Hospital in Moscow, which was described as the premier children's hospital in the nation. The head doctor there took us for a visit to a ward where there were forty children suffering with leukemia. She told of the difficulty of trying to help the children without proper drugs. A cart about two feet by four feet in size sat at the entrance of the ward, and she explained that the packages of medicine stacked on top of the cart had been sent from Germany. Received two days before our visit, these drugs were the only ones she had, and when they were gone, her supply would be empty.

Standing in the ward where the forty girls, some from the Chernobyl area, were being treated, she pointed to an instrument on a stand and said that was the only infusion machine she had among all of these patients. When the doctor left the room, she asked me to walk down the hall with her where she said that she wanted to talk to a bishop. Her conversation centered on the hard choice which she had to make in light of the shortage of medicine and equipment. How do you choose which child gets the drugs when there are not enough to go around? And who gets the one piece of equipment when many need to have the benefit of its use? These are agonizing decisions for the physician and for a representative of the church. By sending drugs to her hospital, United Methodists had responded again in the name and spirit of Jesus Christ.

The hotel we were assigned to stay in by Intourist, the Soviet travel agency, was out on the edge of the city of Moscow. Upon arriving in the city, arrangements were made for us to stay in the big hotel just off the Kremlin square, which would make it much more convenient for us to see the agencies we had come there to visit. There was a woman at the desk of that hotel who made this convenience possible, and Dr. Nugent wanted to reward her for her help. Before leaving New York he had asked a Russian woman what gift items would be most prized by Russians to whom we might wish to express appreciation for their helpful service. The item at the top of the list for women was pantyhose, and the general secretary came prepared with several pairs of pantyhose in various sizes. One morning he wanted to reward the lady at the desk downstairs who had made it possible for us to stay in this more convenient hotel. There was a problem. We had never seen her standing up. She was always seated in a chair behind the counter. Dr. Nugent went downstairs, engaging her in conversation, during which he attempted to peer over the counter to see if he could determine the size of pantyhose he ought to give her. Many are the tasks of the general secretary of the General Board of Global Ministries! We did not find out if the size he selected was the right one, but the gift was right, as was evident by the expression of delight on her face when she opened the package.

One night the phone rang in my hotel room sometime between three and four o'clock in the morning. It was Dr. Nugent calling. He has the habit of carrying a shortwave radio in his luggage wherever he travels in the world. That morning he was calling to tell me that the Gulf War had started. He was listening to a radio broadcast originating from Tel Aviv where the radio announcer was watching the CNN television broadcast and was describing what he was seeing of the invasion. Randy spent several minutes relaying to me the radio announcer's description of the television pictures.

Perhaps this desire to want always to be in touch, even if it means carrying a shortwave radio around the world, is the reason he always seems to me to be the best-informed person about what is happening in the world of anyone with whom I have ever been associated.

GBGM at its spring meeting in 1991 heard the report of our visit to

Moscow and voted an initiative of mission response to the Soviet Union. On a second visit to Moscow in December on behalf of the Board, Dr. Nugent and I made contacts to follow up the beginning of this initiative.

One purpose of this visit was to continue to cultivate a relationship with the patriarch of the Russian Orthodox Church. Dr. Nugent was given special attention by the patriarch on this visit. An invitation to the patriarch's personal residence in a wooded section outside the city of Moscow was a sign of the patriarch's regard for Dr. Nugent as a church leader. I thought that when the patriarch at this meeting spread caviar on toast and handed it to Dr. Nugent, it must have been a first for United Methodists.

The second significant action taken on this second visit to Moscow was contact with Naina Yeltsina, the wife of Soviet President Boris Yeltsin. The United Methodist Committee on Relief (UMCOR) had need of some building space to aid in its humanitarian aid program. Building space was at a very great premium—very difficult to locate and extremely expensive. Arrangements had been made for a visit with Mrs. Yeltsin. The afternoon of the visit, a room had been arranged in our hotel and proper refreshments secured.

A few minutes before Mrs. Yeltsin was expected to arrive, a representative of her security force came to say it had been decided that the security of the hotel was not adequate for Mrs. Yeltsin's safety. This seemed strange because the hotel was in the walls of an old monastery and seemed to be the most secure of all the hotels in Moscow.

The security officer indicated that other arrangements would be made for a visit with Mrs. Yeltsin the following morning in a government building. Then, as if to make amends for the last-minute cancellation of the meeting with the president's wife that afternoon, the man gave Dr. Nugent and me an invitation from Mrs. Yeltsin to be the Yeltsins' guests at the Bolshoi Theatre that night and to be escorted and hosted by their daughter, Tonya Yeltsin.

I have seen Dr. Nugent with presidents and kings in several places of the world and have always found him to be an extremely effective, efficient, and competent representative of The UMC. That night as we sat center stage in the second row of the beautiful awe-inspiring building with tiers of boxes reaching to the high ceiling, I thought that our general secretary, ever so competent in worldwide relations, was about to be the center of an international incident. The music had been playing for no more than five minutes when I noticed that Dr. Nugent was asleep in the second row front center sitting with the president's daughter. Fortunately this did not turn out to be a source of international embarrassment. In fact after wondering how he could fall asleep, the next thing I knew it was intermission and I became aware that the bishop had joined the general secretary in a nap in a very public place! The explanation for this, although not an acceptable excuse, may have been that we were up each night very late on the phone with our offices in the United States doing follow-up for the negotiations that we had been engaged in during the daytime.

The next morning, word was sent that Mrs. Yeltsin would see us at ten o'clock. Dr. Nugent had a visit scheduled with the representative of the education section of the Russian Orthodox Church, and so it was decided that I would lead the visit to the office of the president's wife. She was very gracious in her welcome and expressed appreciation for the work The UMC had begun in Russia. I have to observe that she was a very direct negotiator for the use of the building space we had come there to obtain. She always wanted to know specifically what the Russian people would receive in return. I was pleased during the visit with Mrs. Yeltsin that she indicated her interest in helping with the work of UMCOR.

At one point in the conversation she paused and for a moment changed the subject. Through the interpreter she said to me, "We are looking forward to the visit of President and Mrs. Clinton in a few weeks." She paused and then said "And bishop, you know that she is a United Methodist." Of course I knew, but I was surprised that Mrs. Yeltsin knew and that she made this connection between our conversation and the United States president's wife.

It so happened that a few months following that conversation, I had an unplanned and unexpected meeting with Mrs. Clinton on a street in Copenhagen where she had gone to make a speech for a United Nations conference. When I told Mrs. Clinton about Mrs. Yeltsin's remarks, she expressed delight that the Russian President's wife knew her church connection.

The highlight of this second visit to Moscow on behalf of the Board was the opportunity to visit the Sunday morning worship of the First United Methodist Church in Moscow. The congregation gathered in the assembly room of a large apartment complex. To have the opportunity to see the people gather, to hear the singing of the hymns, to hear the Christmas Scriptures read was a thrilling experience, considering that only a few months before there had been no United Methodist work in the Russian capital. The Reverend Ludmilla Gorbazova, the pastor of this Moscow church, is a remarkable woman who helped to lead the singing at Global Gathering III of the Board in Kansas City in 1997, and in 1998–1999 she was in Nashville translating some of the hymns in *The United Methodist Hymnal* into Russian.

The Sunday we visited her church in Moscow, her daughter told us that Reverend Gorbazova had a medical problem and asked if she could be helped. We made arrangements for her to go home with us to Houston, where she received medical treatment at Methodist Hospital. She lived with us during the two weeks before Christmas that year in our residence in Houston while waiting for her surgery at Methodist Hospital. One of the fond memories that we have of that Christmas is the picture of her playing the grand piano in our living room with our grandchildren standing around as she filled the house with Christmas music.

The immediate effect of the Russia Initiative was to result in humanitarian aid being extended to the Soviet people. This was quickly followed by the appointment of a bishop in Moscow and the establishment of churches. Within a few years, several scores of churches had been organized.

Highlighting Evangelism

Another new activity came from a decision made during the 1985–1988 quadrennium to create a cabinet level position for evangelism. During the 1989–1992 quadrennium, the staff person for evangelism was employed and the work on the Committee for Mission Evangelism began.

Although evangelism has always been at the center of the work of mission, the person filling this new staff position would focus and make more visible evangelism in all areas of the Board's work. The position was to produce materials on evangelism, sponsor special events, consult with all of the units of the Board about evangelism interests, and assist with the training of personnel. The position proved to be a very valuable asset for the Board in achieving the goals for which it is responsible.

Establishing the Mission Resource Center

Another major development during the 1989–1992 quadrennium was the establishment in Atlanta of the Mission Resource Center. The Mission Resource Center was located on the campuses of the Interdenominational

Theological Center and Candler School of Theology of Emory University. Here a core curriculum was designed for the training of mission personnel. The curriculum included biblical and theological studies, United Methodist polity and history, evangelism leadership, and experiential/contextual learning. Missionaries who had served in the field somewhere in the world, resource people from the seminaries, and visiting church leaders from other countries were on the faculty used at the center. The first class of persons arrived in Atlanta in January 1990. The three-month training period would provide the initial orientation about the purpose of our mission activity as well as information about the realities one might face on the mission field.

In addition to academic buildings, the center had the use of an apartment complex on the campus of Emory University. The availability of these apartments created a community for these persons who shared similar commitments, and although their assignments might be in different parts of the world, it created an enriching environment for sharing, learning, and worshiping together. This arrangement also made it possible for the whole family of those with spouses and children to receive training together. The training course offered an orientation to understanding the mission philosophy of The UMC, along with Bible study and some exposure to what mission means in today's world. Attention was also given to the study of the geographic area to which the mission personnel were to be assigned.

The center has served in a major way an almost unexpected need. Because of civil conflicts that have erupted in many parts of the world, mission personnel have had to be evacuated. In its early days the center played a vital role in the re-entry and debriefing of missionaries who had been assigned to Liberia and the Democratic Republic of the Congo (then Zaire) but because of civil conflict had to be withdrawn. So the center in Atlanta became a facility of temporary refuge for these displaced mission persons, and these people have made a valuable contribution to the whole training community by sharing their experience and the insights gained through their years of service.

There have been persons from some of our affiliated autonomous churches who have lived at the center and given valuable assistance in the training. This has given the center an enriching environment which has helped to provide interactive training through the sharing of what it means to be in mission and to work as a Christian believer in settings of different cultures.

Witnessing and Healing in Africa

The new work in Russia was followed by a mission thrust in Senegal where the Board responded to additional opportunities for ministry which came with changing times.

An inspiring story of progress comes from the church in Mozambique where during this quadrennium the church celebrated its centennial. Going into the 1990s, the nation had experienced many years of civil strife following independence from Portugal. The UMC in that country faithfully maintained its witness during those trying times.

A significant event took place on Easter 1989, when a large church building near the center of the capital city of Maputo was consecrated.

The Africa Church Growth and Development Program raised money to be used to advance the churches in all of Africa. Usually these monies were divided to finance several projects in different countries, but the year before the consecration of the church in Maputo, the delegates to the meeting of Africa Church Growth and Development committed to use all of the funds available for a single project. As a sign of solidarity with the people of Mozambique and as a symbol of the place of The UMC in the search for peace that would offer hope for a better future, all the money would be given to The UMC in Mozambique.

This unselfish decision on the part of the delegates from other countries in Africa made possible the construction of a church building on land strategically located near the center of a capital city. Dr. Nugent and I were present on Easter Sunday, 1989, to participate in the consecration of this structure.

This was during a difficult time for the nation. The countryside was unsafe for travel outside of the larger cities. We could not travel overland from the capital city to the United Methodist Hospital at Chicuque for fear of armed attack along the way. Another mission hospital located several miles from Chicuque had been overrun by bandit forces a short time before, and a number of people were killed at that location. Those who serve Chicuque Hospital were examples of many heroic persons who serve with great compassion and give a Christian witness under very difficult and threatening circumstances in many nations.

The day we flew from Maputo to Chicuque in a mission plane, I noticed that we were flying out over the water of the Indian Ocean. I asked the pilot why we were flying so far off shore, and his reply was that over the water, no one would take a shot at our airplane.

At the hospital, casualties from the fighting were received almost daily, and some days the fighting was so close to the hospital grounds the gunfire could be heard there. The hospital is located in a beautiful site on the Indian Ocean bordered by sandy shores and by palm trees blowing in the breeze of the sea. A missionary doctor from India took us on a tour of the hospital buildings. Men's, maternity, and children's wards and a ward for contagious diseases were all in separate buildings.

We went into a girl's ward in the children's building. Three of the four patients there had been hurt because of the activity connected with the civil strife. One girl about ten years of age had been burned when the vehicle she was riding in with her family had been stopped on a rural road. After the passengers were robbed, they were given a choice of either getting out of the vehicle, in which case they were likely to be machine-gunned, or to stay in the vehicle, which was then set afire. This girl had been burned over most of her body inside the vehicle.

Another child had been cut with a bayonet when bandit forces overran her village.

The third girl who had been hurt in the fighting had her mother beside her bed. With the doctor acting as translator, she gave us a vivid picture of the day that her child was hurt.

Bandit forces came to the village and all the people fled to the bush. The mother thought her daughter was somewhere in the group. Instead of going with the others to the bush, however, the little girl, who was about six years of age, went to hide in her hut. She was not discovered, and when she no longer heard voices outside of the hut, believing that she was safe, she came out of the hut to find her folk.

What she did not know was the bandits had left landmines in the dirt around the village. She stumbled over one of these mines. The explosion mangled both of her legs. She was alone, terrified with fear, and experiencing terrible pain. Her mother told us that the daughter had said that she thought at that moment that "if I could get to the Methodist place [meaning Chicuque Hospital] they would take care of me." Unable to walk, she began pulling herself along the ground on her elbows in the direction of the United Methodist Hospital. She had crawled about two miles along the way when she was found and carried the remaining distance to the hospital.

Part of both of her legs had to be amputated. This terrible story illustrates for me the task of our ministry and mission. To care for those who are alone, hurt, and afraid is the task of Christian mission. In addition,

GBGM is also committed to work without ceasing to alleviate the systemic causes of human suffering.

Almost a decade later, I returned to Mozambique, and what a transformation had been achieved by the citizens of that country! Peace had been accomplished. A symbol of that peace was a program inaugurated as part of the peace process whereby guns could be turned in for tools — hammers, saws, plows.

On this latter visit, the president of the country, whom I had met at the time of my first visit there in 1989, asked me to describe the changes which I now saw in the nation. Among all of the changes which were very evident, I told him I would have to say that the greatest was seen in the expression on the faces of the people. In their eyes, the expression of fear and confusion had been replaced by an expression of hope and anticipation.

Celebrating Landmarks

The work of GBGM is a continual stream of ministry with a heroic past and a challenging future. The 1989–1992 quadrennium saw the celebration of landmarks in the continual journey of the people faithful to God. In 1990, United Methodist Women concluded their centennial era celebration at their assembly attended by 10,000 women in Kansas City. The centennial year of the churches in Peru, Mozambique, and Indonesia were observed. Many annual conferences joined in the celebration of the fiftieth anniversary of UMCOR. The twentieth anniversary of the Black Community Developers and the Indigenous Community Developers were also observed.

The twenty-fifth anniversary of the 1964 agreements which restructured the mission agency were observed during the spring board meeting of 1989. In 1988, the Women's Division had celebrated the twenty-fifth anniversary of the Church Center for the United Nations. Using a special centennial fund, this division enabled underwriting such programs as "Higher Education for Women in Africa" and a series of "Working Conferences of Methodist Women" to strengthen the ministry with and advocacy for women and children in the United States and around the world. In 1990, the World Program Division of the Board joined in marking the tenth anniversary of the Africa Church Growth and Development Program. In the 1980s church membership in Africa more than doubled. Funds had been provided for scholarships to more than one hundred stu-

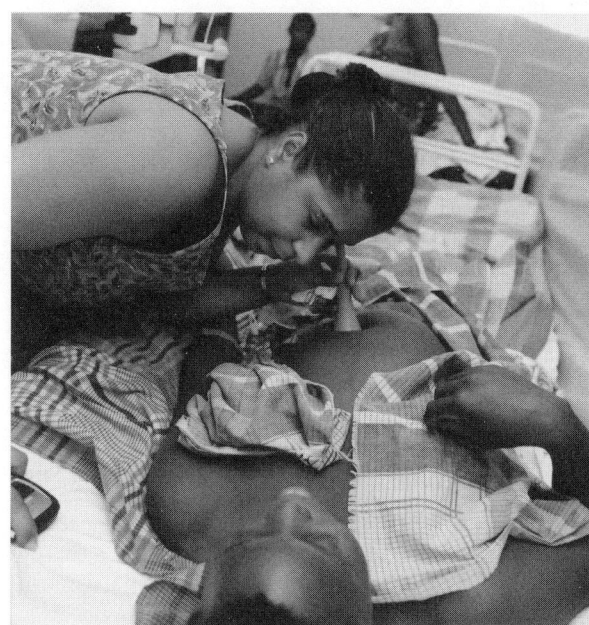

Those who served at the hospital at Chicuque, Mozambique, during the conflict in that country continued to minister to people despite hardships and dangers to their own lives. *(Photo by Richard Lord)*

dents and the construction of more than one hundred church buildings or renovations as well as funds for agriculture, nutrition, and skill development programs through the Africa Church Growth and Development Program.

In 1989, receipts from the Advance for Christ reached more than $30 million, and among the people aided were the victims of Hurricane Hugo. In 1990, about 2,500 designated projects in one hundred countries were funded through the Advance.

One of the enjoyable and rewarding outcomes of being president of GBGM was the opportunity to work with Dr. Randolph Nugent. The general secretary is a world citizen and has the wide interest and knowledge of a true renaissance man. During the time we worked together he was president of the Africa American Association, and we traveled together to one of their meetings in Zambia. The association performs the extremely valuable service of providing an informal forum where leaders of government in Africa and the United States can meet and, off the record, discuss problems of mutual interest. It was a high tribute to Dr. Nugent that he had been elected president of this group.

Also active in the association was Maurice Tempelsman, who sometimes had the leaders of the association meet on his yacht on the East River. Since Mr. Tempelsman was frequently the escort of Jacqueline Kennedy Onassis, Dr. Nugent related to me with a chuckle that on the night of such meetings his two daughters would scheme to get an invitation to go with him so that they could see Ms. Onassis.

Dr. Nugent is also active in work nationally for the benefit of persons with AIDS. Elizabeth Taylor is active in that organization and came to know Dr. Nugent through that connection. He was invited to attend her big birthday party in Florida one year. When Ms. Taylor learned that he did not plan to attend, she personally called him to implore his attendance.

When he is in New York on the same night the New York Knicks are playing, you will find him in his seat at Madison Square Garden. He reads extensively, reading books on history, biography, and current events. Such is the nature of our renaissance general secretary.

To have the opportunity to see the massive number of programs that United Methodist people make possible through GBGM in the spirit of Jesus Christ and in recognition of God's call to be concerned, compassionate, and loving towards one's neighbor is awesome to behold. As I have said before, one mind is not large enough to comprehend it all. We can just be thankful that God has called us to be a servant people to all of God's creation.

CHAPTER 4

Years of Initiative for Mission
F. Herbert Skeete (1993–1996)

*F*ROM MY VANTAGE point as president of the General Board of Global Ministries (GBGM), 1993–1996, I was able to work more closely with the Reverend Dr. Randolph Nugent, general secretary, as friend and colleague. The accomplishments of those last four years will give a global picture of our United Methodist Church (UMC) in its far-reaching service to our ever-changing world. Much of this information is taken from my annual reports to the Board as its president.

Developing Dialogues and New Structure

In my first address to the Board, I said that the full embrace of mission requires active witness modeled on the life of Jesus Christ through faith, the humbling and emptying of selves, taking the form of servanthood even as Jesus did. Mission means taking up residence where and as people live, living with and on behalf of others for the sake of the life abundant. I suggested four objectives for the quadrennium:

(1) Cost reductions, including that of the semiannual meetings of directors; (2) greater director concentration on policy rather than attempts to micromanage; (3) development of new partnerships with annual and central conferences; and (4) achievement of a servant ministry.

These goals were largely met by two significant efforts on the part of the Board: First, by the end of the quadrennium, dialogues had been held in every annual conference; the central conferences in Europe, Africa, and the Philippines; the three missionary conferences (Alaska, Red Bird, and Oklahoma Indian); and the Spanish-language Rio Grande Conference. Directors and staff listened to the concerns of the leadership in these conferences and laid plans to respond to them. Among the major themes were strengthening the mission volunteer program, increased opportunities for local church participation in mission, including children and youth, and greater focus on mission education.

Second, sensing the need for more efficiency and a more responsive organization, the Board proposed a new structure for itself to the General Conference of 1996. The plan had several important features. All units were to be global in scope. The Board was conceived of as a partner with annual conferences and autonomous churches in mission. Internally the units were organized to work in teams. The number of directors was reduced from 180 to 90, half the size, resulting in great savings for the semiannual board meetings and committee meetings. We were glad General Conference approved this plan, which was ready to be put into effect in 1996.

Implementing Initiatives

The initiatives and accomplishments for the quadrennium included:

Eastern Europe

When I began as president of the Board in the fall of 1992 (officers for boards are elected in the last fall of the quadrennium, and the new quadrennium begins officially the next January), we knew we could build on the work our predecessors had done. One of the initiatives of the previous quadrennium had been the mission to Russia. Little did we realize how tumultuous and challenging this period would be in the life of Russia. Not only were the political and economic orders in constant upheaval, but the Russian Orthodox Church was having to make its own adjustment to this period.

We did have our church registered in Russia and by the end of the quadrennium we had ordained twelve deacons and thirteen local pastors. The Moscow Theological Seminary was organized with relations to four United Methodist seminaries in the United States. United Methodist congregations and institutions were established in thirty locations.

We also saw the historic witness of Methodism in other former Eastern bloc countries renewed and expanded. Three Latvian congregations recovered property and were redeveloped. What is called the oldest Methodist congregation in the old Russian Empire, dating from 1900, in Kaunas, Lithuania, was reorganized. Some surviving members of the congregation were present. We began collecting funds for the construction of two centers in Estonia, the Baltic Mission Center in Tallinn and the Agape Center in Parnu. Three missionaries were assigned to Bulgaria, the first U.S. Methodist or United Methodist missionaries there in fifty years.

Along with all this activity, the World Program Division established a new area office for Europe that included Russia.

Kazakhstan

The end of the Cold War brought more open relations between the U.S. and countries of the former Soviet Union, including a greater sharing of the effects of nuclear weapons testing on human populations and the natural environment. The Board convened two scientific dialogues on this issue during the quadrennium, one in Kazakhstan and the second in the U.S.

A major topic was the effect of forty years of testing by the governments of the U.S. and Soviet Union. To foster ongoing cooperation and communication, the Board established in 1995 the U.S.–Kazakhstan International Foundation on Radiation, Ecology and Health. The foundation was intended to be a repository of research materials on the results of nuclear blasts at the Semipalatinsk test grounds and to organize forums on the health effects of radiation.

African Church Growth

The civil conflict in Burundi broke out in 1993, hindering our efforts to support the African churches. Many pastors, laypersons, and Africa Church Growth and Development scholars were killed. Nevertheless, the Board continued to press forward with support in the form of the Bishops' Appeal and Campaign for Africa, with relief efforts, and with continued work to start new churches and assist African conferences in their mission.

We had to meet a refugee crisis, with people moving from Burundi and Rwanda into the Democratic Republic of the Congo (then Zaire). At Goma, in eastern Zaire, we set up a temporary village serving Zairean and Rwandan street children. Although this ministry was not permitted to continue because of continued warfare, we saved lives and rescued some children and worked as long as we were able.

Following our disciplinary mandate "to discern those places where the gospel has not been heard," we established a new mission in Senegal. Missionaries were sent to this predominantly Muslim country for the first time.

At the height of the conflict in the former Zaire in 1994, United Methodists provided tents and survival supplies to refugees at Goma. *(Photo by Jeneane Jones)*

With all these efforts, the church in Africa continued to grow. In 1982 African United Methodist churches had 435,000 members. By 1994 they had more than 1,240,000. One of the most creative developments was the way the African churches reached out to one another. The church in Zimbabwe reached into South Africa and Malawi. The church in Zaire reached into Zambia and Tanzania. The church in Angola related to United Methodists in Namibia. New churches were developed in Uganda and Kenya.

New Churches in Latin America

The Board worked with the Council of Evangelical Methodist Churches in Latin America to develop new relationships in several countries, including Colombia, Venezuela, and Nicaragua. We began to plant new congregations in these countries.

New Churches in Asia

Teams explored mission possibilities in Cambodia, Vietnam, Laos, and Thailand. The Indochina United Methodist Caucus in the United States aided in this work.

Hate Crimes and Violence

The bombing of the federal building in Oklahoma City in 1995 dramatized the potent combination of hate and violence. The Board contributed the first $100,000 to a special Advance to rebuild the First United Methodist Church of Oklahoma City, badly damaged by the blast. Members of the Rural Chaplains Association were convened for training sessions on how to counteract and transform organized hate. (One of the contacts of the bombers in Oklahoma City had been in a farmers' group in Michigan.) The Women's Division developed a consideration of hate and violence in its regional schools of Christian mission. We also had a special consultation in 1995, bringing together leading specialists and church leaders on how to respond to this issue. As a result of this meeting we developed several new ways to work with communities and congregations on hate and violence.

Relief Work in Bosnia

The United Methodist Committee on Relief (UMCOR) began work in 1993 in areas that were formerly part of Yugoslavia and broke away. No other church-related agency was on the ground to respond to refugee and other needs. During the next two years, the staff grew to sixty. Among the ministries was a youth house in Zenica. European churches and governments, the U.S. Government, and the United Nations all supported UMCOR's work in Bosnia.

Carrying out General Conference Mandates

Although not exactly a mandate, the action of the 1992 General Conference in voting by a narrow margin to move the Board from New York exerted pressure on the Board. The Board tried in good faith to respond to requests from the committee that had been formed for information on costs, transportation, employment of a diverse work force, and other questions. The 1996 General Conference, after considering costs and other issues, decided to let the Board remain in New York. But I mention this issue because it did require many hours and meetings and much travel on my part and the part of other members of the Board during the quadrennium.

That same 1992 General Conference gave the Board several large responsibilities:

National Plan for Hispanic Ministry

By the end of the quadrennium, a total of 450 lay missioners, 200 pastor/mentors, and 95 facilitators and trainers were in place. In addition, 51 new Hispanic congregations had been started in 17 annual conferences, 220 faith communities had been established in 35 annual conferences, and 337 community or outreach ministries had been started in 36 annual conferences.

Special Program on Substance Abuse and Related Violence

Responding to the continued evil of drug addiction, the Board worked with the Council of Bishops and the General Board of Church and Society. Programs were developed to train congregations and communities to prevent drug/alcohol abuse and violence. Demonstration projects were held in five states. Training was provided for key lay missioners working in the Native American Comprehensive Plan and the National Hispanic Plan.

Communities of Shalom

Pioneered in seven communities in the Los Angeles area, this program focused on spiritual renewal, congregational development, community economic development, health care, and the strengthening of racial and class ties. More than 250 urban and rural communities in 16 annual conferences in the U.S. and one in Africa engaged in this program.

Homelessness

When General Conference passed a resolution on homelessness, the Board realized that local churches and communities were already doing much to help the homeless. Therefore the Board surveyed and assessed existing ministries and built a data bank on them. The Board saw its role as assisting those in the best position to help—local United Methodist churches.

The HIV/AIDS Epidemic

Again, after General Conference decided to continue the Interagency Task Force on HIV/AIDS, the Board was aware that much good work was already being done at the local and regional level. It built an electronic network of churches and individuals working on this issue. This network supported the Covenant to Care program, which is a congregation-based ministry providing Christian welcome and love to persons with HIV/ AIDS and their families. To consider the international aspects of the issue, more than 400 church leaders took part in consultations in Brazil, Zimbabwe, India, and the U.S.

Native American Comprehensive Plan

The Board served as administrator for a national task force that worked on congregational development, leadership development, encounter with Native American spirituality, and denominational presence among Native Americans. Ten trainers were prepared for congregational development. Discussions were begun with seminaries on the ordination of Native American pastors.

Asian-American Language Ministry

The Board was asked to provide staff for a study on the ten different Asian-language ministries in The United Methodist Church. The study resulted in proposals for Asian-language ministries. Specific recommendations were made to the 1996 General Conference, shaped to meet the needs of those in each language group.

Ministry to the Deaf

Support of the National Committee on Deaf Ministries was assigned to the Board for support. The committee did research and found that even though more than 5,000 UM churches offered amplification in their services of worship, fewer than 1,500 offered any other kind of assistive listening device for hard-of-hearing persons. Fewer than 200 offered any type of sign language interpretation for worship, Christian education, or counseling. The committee made a broad range of recommendations to the 1996 General Conference, including annual conference training in deaf ministries and recruitment of deaf, deafened, and hard-of-hearing persons for ordination. The committee also pointed out that annual conferences could offer a good example by making annual conference sessions accessible to the deaf.[1]

These are only a few of the multitude of ministries and actions of a Board that has sought to embody the spirit and the know-how of United Methodists in mission. Many other ministries not mentioned remained vital to people in need: the Advance, in which United Methodists regularly give $25–30 million over and above their regular giving for special needs;

some one hundred community and institutional ministries across the United States; the amazing responsiveness of UMCOR to disasters, which besides those already reported in Bosnia and Oklahoma City included Hurricanes Andrew, Luis, and Marilyn, and the earthquake in Kobe, Japan; and the United Methodist Women's Assembly in Cincinnati in 1994, where 12,000 women met, and the Global Gathering in Indianapolis in 1993, where more than 4,000 participated, both these events marked by prayer, worship, and much reflection on what mission means in our day.

When I began as Board president, I expressed the hope that as a church we could abandon the divisive, negative patterns of recent years and see a more constructive approach to mission. I hoped that we would be led by the Spirit and join in participation with indigenous leaders on every continent. By the end of my period of service, I realized we had made a start on fulfilling these hopes. United Methodists have a passion for mission and we will not rest until we have gone into every corner of the globe and fulfilled the promise of Christ's mission to "make disciples of all nations."

CHAPTER 5

Mission Is Incarnation
Dan E. Solomon (1997–2000)

UNITED METHODISTS BELIEVE in mission! United Methodists support mission! United Methodists are mission initiators and mission sustainers! United Methodists have given and are giving remarkable resources to the General Board of Global Ministries (GBGM). I believe it is a trust well placed.

God's mission happens as a result of the "people plan." God's witness and work in and through the life of Jesus made that remarkably clear. For people of faith, mission is incarnation!

The question before all other questions is "who will go for us?" The "who" question points to incarnation. It must be answered before we proceed to ask the "how" and the "where" questions. The "who" question and not the "why" question is the first question, because God has already answered the "why" question. The "who" question may belong to us, but the "why" question belongs to God! "'For God so loved the world that God gave God's own son, that whoever believes in Him shall not perish, but shall have everlasting life'" (John 3:16, author's paraphrase of New Revised Standard Version).

Mission is not simply something the church does; mission is who the church is! Within GBGM, its directors, staff, and missionary personnel, there is a remarkable and dynamic passion to be the church of Jesus Christ, alive in mission, compassionate in service and care, and leaning into the future that God graciously opens before us.

One of the high privileges of my ministry has been my involvement with GBGM. Through my eight years as a director of the Board, I have been inspired, informed, and challenged by United Methodism's world outlook and outreach. My travels as president of the former World Program

Division, and then as president of the Board, have blessed me with an awareness of the pulse-beat of United Methodist mission witness and service.

No one personifies to me the intensity that characterizes United Methodist mission vitality better than Dr. Randolph Nugent. Whether it be in Spartan settings remote and isolated, on lengthy airline flights, in meetings of the Board and its committees, or in private moments, Randy's conversations with me make it clear that Randy thinks mission, talks mission, plans mission, and anticipates mission.

On more than one occasion Randy has said, "We have a great church. Our people love to be in mission." I cannot help but think that Randy's own "love for mission" is the lens through which he views all of our life together. Perhaps there are times when Randy loves what he want the rest of United Methodism to love, even though United Methodists are hesitant or uncertain about the risks and joys of mission initiatives.

Of this I am sure, Randy has a deep appreciation for and commitment to GBGM. His commitment is not a blind loyalty, but rather a lover's critique. Some of the Board's most significant new initiatives, from simple, behind-the-scenes innovations, to far-reaching and grand endeavors have had their inception or their acceleration because of Randy's desire to see the Board improve its "mission delivery" for The United Methodist Church (UMC).

In the last quadrennium of the century, The UMC achieved goals for mission that it had been striving toward for decades.

Proclaiming the Gospel in New Lands

Seeking to proclaim the gospel in places where it had not been heard, the church established a presence in several countries where it had not been before, leaving only a handful of lands where The UMC does not have a mission.

These countries where a new presence was established included Cambodia, Lithuania, Honduras, and El Salvador. A significant number of new congregations were formed in these countries as well as in Venezuela and Colombia, where initiatives had begun the preceding quadrennium.

In Cambodia more than one hundred congregations were established. Here The UMC in the U.S. cooperated with United Methodist churches in Switzerland and France and Methodist churches in Korea and Singapore. Together these churches sent seventeen missionaries to Cambodia.

In Lithuania six new United Methodist congregations were established in a church whose revival began in the early 1990s. In a new congregation being planned in the capital, Vilnius, worship and ministry will be done in four languages: Lithuanian, Polish, Russian, and English. Four GBGM missionaries and a United Methodist Committee on Relief (UMCOR) consultant were assigned to Lithuania.

In Honduras, a new congregation came into being in July 1998, and by the end of the year it had more than one hundred members. New communities of faith were also begun in San Salvador, the capital of El Salvador, and an outlying area. Two new churches were started in Colombia, making four Methodist congregations there. In Venezuela and Nicaragua leadership was trained in cooperation with autonomous churches in Latin America, with the intent to form new congregations.

Various ministries were continued, many with missionary presence, in such new settings as Ukraine, Kazakhstan, Kaliningrad, Azerbaijan, the Republic of Georgia, the Czech and Slovak republics, the other Baltic countries, Hungary, Romania, and all of the Balkan countries. Where a missionary could not be sent, the church worked through relief and other ministries.

In other Asian countries United Methodism continued to work in Indonesia, where the Gereja Methodist Indonesia consisted of 276 churches, 248 preaching posts, 157 ordained pastors, and hundreds of lay speakers who serve 40,183 full members and 49,913 potential members. The church also worked in Laos, Nepal, Malaysia, Myanmar, and Afghanistan.

Although the church was already present in most African countries, in this quadrennium United Methodism developed the foothold established in 1995 in Senegal. Senegal is a Muslim country with prohibitions on proselyting, yet United Methodist missionaries have formed several worshiping communities and purchased property for the first United Methodist church building there.

New congregations were also planted in Namibia, Botswana, Malawi, Guinea, Burundi, Rwanda, Uganda, the Sudan, and Kenya. These efforts have contributed to Africa's leadership in becoming the fastest-growing area for Methodism in the world.

These efforts, combined with new congregations in a host of countries on every continent, demonstrate that United Methodists never cease to explore new opportunities in which to seek converts to Jesus Christ.

Recruiting and Placing More Missionaries

Every year from 1996 to 2000 saw the number of missionaries supported by The UMC increase:

1996	950
1997	963
1998	1,047
1999	1,763
2000	2,180

Since 1991, our church has sent mission personnel to twelve new countries, including Bulgaria, Bosnia, Cambodia, Kazakhstan, Lithuania, Papua New Guinea, Palestine, Russia, Tanzania, Uganda, Zambia, and Senegal.

The first Korean-American mission pastors were commissioned in 1997, enabling the church to channel the spiritual energy of Korean Americans into creative areas.

GBGM created Missioners of Hope in 1998 to enable Africans as well as North Americans to serve as missionaries. By March 2000, one hundred and three Missioners of Hope had been commissioned.

Another new program, the Bishop W. T. Handy, Jr., Young Adult Missioners, was also created in 1998 with the goal of enlisting 800 young adults across the global church in mission.[1]

The deaconess program was also revitalized in 1998, and after several years when none or only one or two deaconesses were consecrated, eight were consecrated in 1999.

The UMC perseveres in making vivid the call of God for men and women to serve as missionaries throughout the world.

Responding to Critical Areas of Need

Mission is more than numbers. Mission is following Jesus in taking risks to be servants to all. In this last quadrennium GBGM has responded to crises and new issues that have risen in the U.S. and other parts of the globe.

Hate and violence have erupted with destructive force, with children killing children, and African Americans, gays, and others subjected to outright murder and the burning of churches.

Ethnic cleansing has become a contemporary euphemism for genocide. Disproportionately high numbers of racial/ethnic persons have been sent

Sunday school teacher and music leader Thom Sinath (center) and members of Khnar Thmei United Methodist Church in Siem Reap, Cambodia, perform a traditional Cambodian dance with a hymn written by church members to welcome visitors. *(Photo by Linda Worthington, United Methodist News Service)*

to prison and executed. The Ku Klux Klan and other hate groups have openly communicated on the world wide web. In the midst of these terrible developments, the church has once again actively witnessed to the God of love, reconciliation, peace, and justice.

The UMC contributed money and large numbers of volunteers to rebuild the churches that were burned. United Methodist Women (UMW) was especially notable for its leadership in helping to educate the church on hate crimes and violence. UMW worked to strengthen hate crime laws and to pursue universal human rights. Restorative Justice was established as a program that would go beyond traditional prison ministries to embrace reconciliation of victims and criminals.

UMCOR is renowned for acting promptly and efficiently to assist those affected by natural disasters. It certainly did this extremely well in responding to disasters in the U.S., Central America, and Asia in these years. But it has done more, especially in the countries where ethnic conflict raged with such fury that millions were killed and more millions were maimed and persecuted. UMCOR was instrumental in trying to relieve human suffering in the midst of the conflict in Rwanda, Burundi, and the Democratic Republic of the Congo. It channelled volunteers, food, medicine, and other supplies to refugees there.

In Bosnia and again in Kosovo, UMCOR began its work of rebuilding areas torn by war. Soon the U.S. Government was so impressed that it asked UMCOR to be the instrument for U.S. aid in delivering humanitarian relief and carrying out long-term development. When countries go to war, they excel in destruction. It is left for others to do the hard work of rebuilding and reconciliation. In addition to the U.S. Government agencies who have been donors, many nongovernmental organizations (NGOs) also used UMCOR. These nongovernmental organizations included the United Nations (UN), Action by Churches Together, Christian Aid United Kingdom, Swiss Ecumenical Church Aid, Dutch Inter-Church Aid, Conference des Églises, the Women's Division of GBGM, and Christoffel-Blindenmission.

The NGO program allowed the church to maximize its mission efforts in a dramatic way. In 1998 an investment of less than $1.5 million by the church returned more than $12.2 million in grants. These grants made the difference between life and death for individuals, families, and communities seeking to overcome the ravages of war.

One of the most insidious weapons of contemporary warfare is the land mine. The UN estimates that it would take 1,000 mine-clearing personnel more than 30 years to discover and disarm the 6 million mines planted in Bosnia and Croatia. In Angola there are 9 million land mines, equal to the population of the country. Of the 69 countries affected, some 26,000 deaths or injuries occur annually, and one-third of these victims are children.

GBGM initiated an anti-land mine program in 1999. Mozambique was the first country to be considered. Military and engineering experts and humanitarian activists were part of a task force that searched for state-of-the art technology to remove land mines. United Methodists with specialized skills who can assist in this effort were recruited. The Board already had a very effective rehabilitation program in Angola that provided affordable prosthetics to victims. This program was to be expanded and used in other countries.

Another crisis in the last years of the century was the U. S. Government

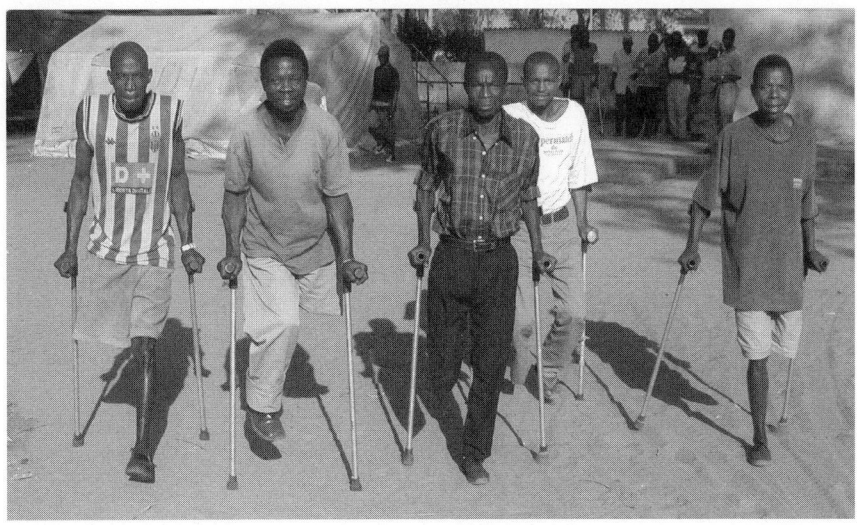

These victims of land mines in Angola are among 86,000 who have been harmed by the mines, made in more than twenty-two countries, used in Angola. *(Photo by Paul Jeffrey, United Methodist News Service)*

policy on welfare. Although The UMC represents within its membership a cross-section of voters who have been voting to change welfare policies, the church is united in its concern for the impact of these policies on the most vulnerable people in our society. To that end community centers related to the church increased the intensity of their services to persons being moved from welfare to self-support. UMW enhanced its traditional concern for women, children, and youth with special efforts to ensure the safety and well-being of these groups. UMW also joined the Council of Bishops in its Initiative on Children and Poverty, which continues to educate, advocate, and do direct service on this issue.

Children in Africa also received special attention because of their victimization as a result of wars, disease, and long periods of neglect. The Hope for the Children of Africa Advance Special was created to challenge the church to respond to children orphaned by war, children recruited as soldiers, and children paying the price in disease, hunger, and ignorance for the sins of their elders. This program is now supporting projects in many African countries where these conditions are the worst. The Board again joined the Council of Bishops as it ignited a new effort through its Hope for the Children of Africa appeal to minister to these children.

Expanding Concepts Globally

A number of ministries that have proved effective in the U.S. were expanded to embrace global populations.

Shalom Zones, which grew out of the Los Angeles disturbances in 1992, had already been developed in the preceding quadrennium. The Shalom Zones program sought to establish communities in areas where not only economic development and community organization are needed but also spiritual renewal and reconciliation. The goal for this quadrennium was 300 Shalom sites by the year 2000. But by late 1999, GBGM had helped to create 313 such communities, and new ones were created in Zimbabwe and West Africa as well.

The Rural Chaplaincy program is ecumenical and includes primarily United Methodists but also Roman Catholics, Disciples of Christ, and Presbyterians. These chaplains have traditionally sought to minister to those under stress because of economic disaster, urbanization, and attendant social and spiritual problems. In this quadrennium Rural Chaplains went global and after visits to parts of the former Soviet Union began including members from countries outside the U.S.

Comprehensive community-based primary health care, which has been used in the U.S. to empower low-income populations, has also gone global. A committed couple, Drs. Raj and Mabel Arole, had brought this concept to Jamkhed, India. The Health and Welfare Ministries arm of GBGM asked the Aroles and their colleagues in India to help train people from other global regions in this concept. This they have done, and through the Board low-income people in Bolivia, Venezuela, Angola, Senegal, the Philippines, and China have been trained.

Finding New Methods for New Challenges

The Board has also acted during this quadrennium to make innovations needed by changing circumstances.

After the 1996 General Conference approved a new organization for GBGM, we faced the task of making it work. That task was accomplished in this quadrennium. The Board has streamlined its lines of accountability and eliminated many of the features that impeded mission. The number on the board of directors was reduced to half the previous number, lowering costs and making action and communication much easier. These changes were not merely formal — they had to do with attitudes toward working with the church. One of the major themes has been partnership, which means agency and annual conferences working cooperatively in the name and spirit of Christ.

One new area created by the reorganization was Mission Volunteers. This unit is a resource and clearinghouse for some 54,000 volunteers, more than one thousand per week. Mission volunteers is a movement that is still growing, as United Methodists apply their "hands-on, faith-on, and minds-on" experience to problems in our cities, rural areas, and developing countries.

Another new program was the Millennium Fund for Mission, created to meet the problems of U.S. cities, rebuild post-Communist areas of Europe, and support the growing church in Africa. The innovative aspect of the Millennium Fund was that it used United Methodist funds managed by GBGM to match gifts from others. The loaves and fish multiply when each complements the other.

GBGM contributed $9 million in funds made from investments to launch the Millennium Fund and has challenged all United Methodists to match that amount. Church members also were asked to contribute volunteer time, equipment, and supplies and make promotional efforts for the fund. By early in the year 2000, the $9 million of the Board funds had already been expended.

A good example of how the fund worked came from the United Methodist Church in Geneva, Illinois. A few years ago when the congregation raised $4 million for a building fund, it decided to commit 1 percent of that amount for mission. This $40,000 has now gone to renovate a Methodist church in Kaunas, Lithuania, that had been closed during the Communist era.

Mission includes these and many more ministries of GBGM in this quadrennium. To tell the whole story would take much more space than a single chapter in a book. The Board and the church are continuing the community and institutional ministries, the ministries with persons with AIDS and their families, the research and money for new church buildings, and the United Methodist Development Fund to support new church buildings in the U.S.

This quadrennium the Board took two decisive steps in communications that are generating a sense of true partnership in the church. The first was a series of dialogues with leaders of annual conferences, following up on the suggestions made in the first set of dialogues held earlier. These sessions enabled the annual conferences and the Board to focus on the questions and concerns of all United Methodists so that our mission reflected the whole church. Although we usually think of the second step as less important than the first, in this case the second step was critical, because it gave the Board an opportunity to show good faith in the way it was listening to the church and serving the church.

The other step was entry into the world wide web. This may not seem like very much to those who do not use the web or even a computer. But an increasing number are communicating on the web globally, and no constituency is more affected by it than youth. The church must respond with the most effective methods possible to communicate the gospel. One of the most productive things the Board has done is to give local churches free web space so they can have their own web pages. By the end of the quadrennium more than five thousand United Methodist churches were using the Board's server to host their web pages.

Of course, the Board continued to use traditional methods like this one—print. The Service Center distributed 13 million print pieces and videos, most of them produced by the Board. *New World Outlook*, the award-winning mission magazine of the Board, and *Response*, the journal of the Women's Division, contined to tell the story of ongoing mission with strong photographs and vivid writing. Videos often produced "on site" where mission was taking place continued to be used by the Board to report on current mission and also to motivate people to be in mission. These examples of communication show a spirit of innovation that is vital if we are to fulfill our calling to be Christ's servants in a hungry and growing world. To that end the Board began to explore radio and other means of communication that will figure into how we do mission in the next century.

Devoting the Millennium to Incarnational Mission

A new millennium: the very phrase almost takes our breath away. Isn't it remarkable to be living at this time in history!

Yet, this time in history is not nearly as remarkable as this opportunity in history. God's people have new reason to focus on these days, not as *chronos*—the time measured by the calendar—but as *kairos*—the right time for seizing God's opportunity. As surely as early Christians at the beginning of the first millennium with joy and passion humbly shared the transforming grace of God through Jesus Christ, so we also have that same clear mission as we enter God's gift of a new millennium.

First and foremost, a new millennium is God's time! What we bring to the new millennium is not a superficial party, but rather, a heavenly banquet. GBGM has been called by God and commissioned by United Methodism to address the spiritual and physical hungers of humanity by inviting persons to feast upon the good news of God's love in Jesus Christ and to quench their thirst with the waters of everlasting life.

CHAPTER 6

Endowed by God
Arthur F. Kulah (1993–2000)

*I*N THE APOCRYPHAL book of Ecclesiasticus, the author, in chapter 44, attempts to "praise famous men." The *New English Bible* describes these as "heroes . . . through whom the Lord established his renown and revealed his majesty in each succeeding age" (v. 2). These persons, the writer insists, were "sage counselors . . . with prophetic power" who led through wisdom and knowledge because they were endowed by God.

There are persons in The United Methodist Church (UMC) who aptly fit the description of these faithful and loyal servants of God. Among these outstanding persons is Dr. Randolph Nugent, general secretary of the General Board of Global Ministries (GBGM).

At the dawning of a new century and the third millennium we recognize and celebrate dedicated service to Christ through the church by Dr. Nugent. We honor our dear friend and what he has accomplished to strengthen and magnify the mission of the church, especially as general secretary.

In this essay, not only will we reflect on his years of service, but we will also trace the origin of the Methodist mission in Liberia. Furthermore, we will highlight his role in giving focus to the development of United Methodism, and the programs which emerged as a result of his efforts.

Beginnings of Methodism

Liberia is the pioneering field of United Methodist mission in Africa. The Methodist Church was organized in 1822 on board the ship which brought the earliest settlers from North America to West Africa. The Methodist Church, however, did not spread beyond the coastal areas where the settlers resided until the first Methodist missionary to Liberia arrived in 1833. Melville Cox is credited with formally organizing the Liberia Annual Conference and encouraging the arrival of other missionaries.

Cox lived less than a year before succumbing to a terminal illness. His famous last words, "Though a thousand fall, let not Africa be given up," became not only his epitaph, but a challenge to the church to view Africa as the great frontier for Christian expansion and Liberia as the gateway to the conversion of Africans.[1]

The work of succeeding missionaries will remain indelible on the history of Liberia: Thomas Crozier, Sophia Farrington, John Seys, Bishop and Mrs. Francis Burns, George W. and Winifred Harley, the Reverend U. S. and Vivinnie Gray, Anna Hall, Mr. and Mrs. Charles Price, Robert and Ladonnla Carey, and Paul and Segrun Sundar. Their efforts provided the impetus to Bishop William Taylor who established the church in, what is today, Mozambique, Democratic Republic of Congo, Angola, and Zimbabwe as districts of the Liberia Annual Conference. Bishop Taylor, in his zeal for Africa, is believed to have climbed a mountain near Old Mutare Mission in Zimbabwe. He reportedly had a vision there in which he saw boys and girls going to school at the mission from every corner of Africa. The establishment of Africa University on that site where Bishop Taylor had his vision is a fulfillment of a great prophecy.

The mission of the Methodist Church in Liberia was marked by expansion through the establishment of mission stations which served as outreach centers. For many years Liberia and other countries in Africa remained mission fields served by missionaries from the West (Europe and North America).

In 1981, Dr. Randolph Nugent was elected general secretary of the General Board of Global Ministries. His tenure is marked by many notable achievements, among which are concepts that led to unique programs that have made a significant impact on United Methodism in Africa.

Conceiving New Ways of Mission

Six major Africa-oriented concepts were initiated by GBGM under Dr. Nugent's leadership. First, there were significant efforts to shift the perspective of United Methodists in America away from viewing Africa as a mission field to that of being a full partner in the *body of Christ*. The goal was to establish a new *partnership*. This relationship was characterized by mutuality, a two-way ministry, *and* a friendship of sharing on both sides.

Related to the first concept is the second. This partnership with United Methodists in Africa allowed denominational leaders in Africa to express their aspirations for the growth of the church. In order to accomplish this goal, GBGM sponsored a series of consultations with the annual conferences in Africa. These consultations enabled these conferences to produce long-term planning for their growth and development.

The third concept the Nugent administration promoted was the notion that Africa ought not to be viewed as a continent with problems but as one with potential and possibilities. While the general church often viewed Africa from the perspective of international reports and statistics, the Nugent administration looked at the soul of Africa and began to tap local resources with the belief that The UMC in Africa can contribute significantly to its own growth and development.

The recognition of the role of United Methodism in Africa as negotiator and peacemaker in national conflicts is a fourth concept. Religion plays a vital role in all of life. Consequently, when there are national conflicts the church can ill afford to be a spectator. Instead, the church is called to help broker peace and restore order in society. Dr. Nugent has helped United Methodists in North America to understand more intricately the work undertaken by the leaders of several annual conferences in sub-Saharan Africa to bring peace to their countries. Among the United Methodist bishops of Africa, besides myself, have been Abel Muzorewa of Zimbabwe, Joab Machado of Mozambique, Alfred Ndoricimpa of Burundi, and most recently Joseph Humper of Sierra Leone.

In addition to the aforementioned concepts initiated during the tenure of Dr. Nugent, a fifth concept was to help all United Methodists to know, understand, and appreciate that The UMC in Africa was engaged in several unique methods of evangelism and church growth. In order to propagate the gospel, United Methodists in Africa use the proclamation of Christ not only in formal church settings, but also in schools, clinics, and agricultural projects. When the church undertakes these projects as ministries they are not ends in themselves, but a means to the ultimate end of letting the love of God through Christ be known in the hearts and minds of women, men, and children.

Mission schools have been recognized for producing outstanding lead-

Former Bishop Arthur Kulah continued to lead the Liberia church during a war that was especially harmful to children. *(Photo from General Board of Global Ministries photo library)*

ers for church and society in Africa. President Kwame Nkrumah of Ghana; Kenneth Kaunda, first president of Zambia; Siaka Stevens; and others on the continent were products of mission schools. In Liberia, a significant number of national and church leaders passed through mission schools, including presidents William Tubman and William Tolbert of Liberia, as well as numerous government ministers, ambassadors, managers, business executives, administrators, and various technocrats.

The sixth concept is as foundational as any of the previously discussed concepts. All United Methodists have been called to the awareness that regardless of the location of an episcopal area, bishops give leadership to and serve the interests of the entire global church. The Nugent administration enabled the church to recognize United Methodist bishops in Africa as being more than just African bishops. The resulting perspective is the view of the church as one body, thereby eliminating the idea of Africa as a *mission field.*

These foregoing concepts became policies which guided GBGM and governed its practices in relation to ministry and mission in Africa. Many of these practices took the form of programs. These programs were actually concrete manifestations of the concepts developed under Dr. Nugent's leadership to empower United Methodism in Africa through sustainability, accountability, and proper planning. Five important program initiatives emerged from these concepts.

Emerging Programs

First, there is the establishment of a committee known as *Africa Church Growth and Development*. This committee brings together leaders of the central conferences of Europe and Africa to discuss various dimensions of the church's work in Africa. These include leadership development, evangelism, health, and agriculture. The representatives of the Africa conferences take the lead in determining which projects will benefit from funds that are raised. This is a rare opportunity for African leaders to meet, have dialogue, and set priorities.

Closely related to the African involvement in Africa Church Growth and Development is *the annual meeting of the United Methodist bishops of Africa*. Previously these bishops only met when the Council of Bishops was in session. Through the Nugent administration the bishops meet to respond to the needs and aspirations of The UMC all across Africa.

The reconstruction of the infrastructure of The UMC in Africa has become a major initiative because of large-scale destruction associated with war. *The Millennium Fund for Mission* has become a vital resource to rebuild schools, hospitals, churches, and parsonages. Vital educational and health facilities have long been at the core of UMC mission in Africa.

The fourth program is *an initiative to undergird the pensions* of United Methodist clergy and staff of the annual conferences in Africa. A fund, provided by GBGM but administered by the General Board of Pensions, helps to sustain these church workers during their retirement years.

The final program is known as *Missioners of Hope*. This program is geared towards empowering the children of Africa and transforming their lives so that they may become leaders who serve God, respect humanity, and support the church. Missioners of Hope challenges The UMC in Africa and around the world through the sending of African missionaries to all parts of Africa. It has also provided another means by which the African church has taken major responsibility for the mission of Christ across the continent.

Seeing the African Church in a New Light

Among the many legacies bequeathed to the general church by Dr. Nugent is the equality of all God's children, no matter where they happen to reside. As such, each one has contributions to make to the growth, development, and welfare of The UMC and global society.

The UMC in Africa is seen as a new light. It is no longer merely a church with problems but one of possibilities; it is not a mission field but one with responsibility for leadership in mission; it is not a receiving church but one which has much to give and share with the rest of the world.

The contributions of Dr. Randolph Nugent to the global connection of The UMC can truly be compared to the famous persons described by the writer of Ecclesiasticus. He and his staff were able to accomplish great feats because they were truly *endowed by God*.

CHAPTER 7

Developing a Culture of Mutuality:
The Central Conference of Central and Southern Europe as a Partner in Mission
Heinrich Bolleter (1993–2000)

THE ORIGINS OF The United Methodist Church (UMC) in mainland Europe and in the Balkans go back more than 150 years. An ethnic variety of people migrated to the United States, where they had been converted under Methodist auspices. A continuing problem among them was that of cultural identity. William Nast, for example, one of the German Methodists in Cincinnati, insisted vehemently in his speech at the Methodist Episcopal General Conference of 1860 that German Methodists were no less American than any others. Hundreds of thousands of foreign-born Methodists were brought together in ethnic societies and annual conferences because of their language.

Planting Methodism in Europe

An important spinoff of this ethnic Methodism in America was the planting of the Methodist movement in mainland Europe. Visitors in their home country and officially sent missionaries became the Methodists linking two continents. They must have been the first ones who understood that mission under the umbrella of the Methodist connection can be effective and strong.

There are many stories like the one about the beginnings of the Methodist mission in Strasbourg. The Emperor Napoleon did not allow public meetings, and in private homes not more than nineteen participants were allowed to come together for a family feast. This was a great hindrance for the development of the mission started by Johann Schnatz. Only with the intervention of the American consul in Paris (1868) was permission for the meetings given.

In both the North and South of the United States, foreign missionary societies were formed, including significant societies by women: Methodist Episcopal Church (MEC), 1869; the United Brethren, 1875; the Methodist Episcopal Church, South, 1878; and the Evangelical Association, 1884. Collectively they were supporting the mission on both sides of the Atlantic: Germany, Sweden, Norway, Finland, Denmark, Russia, the Baltic, the Balkans, and France. The mission of the Methodist Episcopal Church in Switzerland, Austria, Hungary, and the northern part of Yugoslavia was initiated by German Methodists, although British Methodists had introduced Methodism to Switzerland in 1777.

Building Infrastructures for Mission

By the end of the 1800s, Methodists on both sides of the Atlantic shared the excitement over the potentialities of missionary opportunities in Europe and the Balkans. Fourteen years later the Western world was embroiled in the first of its global wars. After the First World War the Methodist Episcopal Church, South, entered Belgium, Czechoslovakia, Poland, and Siberia. The U.S. side continued to help building up the infrastructures for the mission: church centers in larger cities and social institutions like orphanages and secondary schools for girls. These were very often sponsored by friends of the foreign missionary societies (like Fanny Gamble-Nast and Gaither Warfield).[1]

On mainland Europe the Methodists were organized as so-called free churches alongside the existing national or state churches (Roman Catholic, Lutheran, Reformed, and Orthodox). The Methodists were and still are in a minority position. The difference between the Methodists and other free churches was and still is that Methodists were ecumenically open and internationally connected. The various branches of our tradition kept the European missions connected to one of the U.S. conferences or jurisdictions. At least the episcopal oversight was provided by an American bishop. Even when some of the annual conferences became self-sustaining, they did not want to cut the ties with the general church.

In October 1925 the Central Conference of Central Europe was constituted under the leadership of Bishop John L. Nuelsen of the MEC. This conference covered at that time annual, provisional, and missionary conferences in northern and southern Germany, Switzerland, Austria, Bulgaria, Hungary, the Baltics, and Russia. This cluster of European conferences came out of the First World War. There were enough reasons to turn away from this fellowship. But Bishop Nuelsen said in the opening address of the newly constituted central conference: "This is a fellowship of faith and hope and love. In the Methodist Episcopal Church we have found our real and deepest task in life. This fellowship brings the uniting and binding strength of the eternal fellowship with God into the dividing and separating powers of humanity. It is stronger than any blood-relation, deeper than national or ethnic relation and more binding than any historically grown solidarity."[2]

Here we can clearly see what is meant by the culture of mutuality that we have developed and would like to strengthen continuously.

In January 1933 the National Socialist party took power in Germany. And in September 1935 when the Central Conference of Central Europe gathered in Freudenstadt, it was announced that the MEC in Germany would constitute a central conference in Germany and elect a German as bishop. And so it happened in 1936, sanctified by the General Conference of the MEC in Columbus, Ohio. The minorities who were cut off had no time for reflection in order to get some ground under their feet. The coming years were marked by the political developments in Europe, by insecurity, war, and the consequences of the Second World War.

Establishing the Conference of Central and Southern Europe

In 1944 Paul N. Garber of The Methodist Church was appointed a bishop of the remnant. In 1945 he moved to Geneva and started to visit the area. He was deeply shocked to see the conditions of the Methodists, who had survived the horrors of the war. It was difficult to imagine that the remnant could constitute a central conference, so it received the status of a provisional central conference.

The General Conference of 1952 in San Francisco gave way to the petition of the Switzerland Annual Conference to form together with all the remaining missions in Central and Southern Europe the "Central Conference of Central and Southern Europe" and elect its own bishop.

The first session took place in Brussels in 1954. Bishop Arthur J. Moore was presiding. He gave the following introduction to the election of a bishop for this area: "Geographically we are in a very vast area and at the same time our Church is comparably small and modest. The future bishop will therefore be faced with an unbelievable big task compared to this small work. It will need more than his knowledge and his strengths, if he really wants to try and make this checkered Central Conference a living body."[3]

(This summary of a very difficult time for the Methodist family in Central and Southern Europe does not cover the experience of the Evangelical and United Brethren churches. In Central and Southern Europe their presence was limited to Switzerland, France, and the western part of Poland, which was formerly German territory. They of course had a significant relationship with the former Evangelical and Brethren churches in Germany proper and assisted greatly in relief after the Second World War.)

Without doubt, the new Central Conference of Central and Southern Europe structure was a helpful tool to build up reciprocal relationships. But the Cold War with the divisions between East and West was hindering the connectional expressions of life tremendously, not to mention the systematic suppression of church life by the Communist governments and their secret services. In some parts of eastern Europe and the Balkans, the church was deprived of its church buildings and the right to conduct youth work or social work. In some places it was even deprived of the right to exist. The culture of mutuality was reduced in many cases to personal relationships. Lay members from the West were the messengers and bridge builders. Unofficial support was brought across the Iron Curtain and in many ways helped the churches to survive. The bishop and the meeting of the executive of the central conference were the visible tools of the connection, and with the exception of Bulgaria all the other conferences behind the Iron Curtain were able to seize the helping hands. Not yet recovered from the wounds of the Second World War, the churches were undergoing a difficult journey of forty years through the Communist wilderness.

Rising from the Ashes of the Post–Cold War

In 1989 when the Berlin wall collapsed and step by step the so-called Socialist countries opened up for a development towards democracy and free market economy, the churches were ready to rise from the ashes and from their lives in the shadow. Mission-oriented, they started to take advantage of the new freedom and to ask for the restitution of their properties. But as poor as they were, they needed help to rebuild the basic infrastructures of the church, to pay the salaries of pastors and the layworkers, and to train new lay missionaries.

One hundred and fifty years have passed since Methodism expanded into the European continent. Ten years have passed since the Cold War came to an end. We are living now in the post–Cold War era. The almost euphoric excitement about the new mission possibilities in the former Socialist countries is confronted with the new realities. Among those are poverty, strife for ethnic and national self-determination, war, and the new difficulties of free traveling in Europe. The rich nations under the Schengen Treaty are asking for visas and building up a new fence against the migrants coming from the East and the South. (The Schengen Treaty established open border zones in countries participating in the European Union.) In all the turbulence, turmoils, wars, and divisions, the Methodist connection was strong enough to endure and overcome. This strength became visible at our district conference meeting in Strumica, Macedonia, in 2000. The speakers for the evenings, which were open to the public, were a Bosnian pastor, a Kosovar layperson, and a representative out of Serbia-dominated Yugoslavia. It became the talk of the town — that the Methodist connection is stronger than all the national and political divisions.

Cultivating and Spreading Mutuality

The Central Conference of Central and Southern Europe together with the General Board of Global Ministries (GBGM) and the General Board of Higher Education and Ministry has initiated a cross-Atlantic dialogue. The theological consultations in the 1980s dealt with questions about the ordained ministry. In 1991 we started a series of international consultations in order to foster an understanding of the complexity of the cultural and political changes in Europe after the end of the Cold War. The Third International Consultation in Vienna was a dialogue on "Church and World at the Beginning of the Third Millennium."

Parallel to this the General Conference allowed more representation of the central conferences on the boards and agencies of the general church. Partnerships and team visits were creating new relationships.

The support of the Women's Division for language study (English and

The Baltic Mission Center in Tallinn, Estonia, was dedicated in 2000 as a place of worship and teaching. *(Photo by Eddie Fox, United Methodist News Service)*

German) is a marvelous contribution to the culture of mutuality. Another helpful link is the European Commission on Mission, where GBGM has its representatives. In this commission, the sending agencies of The UMC in Europe are coordinating their efforts together with partner churches in Africa, Latin America, and Asia. One of the results of this cooperation was the Africa Church Growth and Development Fund, which provided a way for participation of the partner churches in Africa in the planning and setting of priorities in mission.

The culture of mutuality has its own dynamics and works at different levels of togetherness and solidarity. The role of the Methodists in Austria, Switzerland, and, most recently Germany, had rescuing dimensions. GBGM has been and is helping by covering the basic needs of the conferences and churches. Among these actions are: the recent gifts through the Millennium Fund for Mission for pastors' salary support; the reconstruction of the church center in Budapest, Hungary; the new church building in Pilsen Lochotin, Czech Republic (in the last seventy years no new church had been built in this annual conference); the new church center in Sid, Federal Republic of Yugoslavia; the new church center in Varna, Bulgaria; and the conference center in Klarisev, near Warsaw, Poland. Nor should we forget the immense humanitarian aid implemented by the United Methodist Committee on Relief in the Balkans.

These are some insights in the need, the development, and the cultivation of a culture of mutuality within the United Methodist connection. This culture of mutuality is based on the biblical concept of the covenant, "faith working through love," the Methodist affection for structure, the awareness for a global dimension of the church, and the commitment of persons who became the living symbols of connectionalism. Throughout this history, there has been no example of growing mutuality without the leaders functioning as catalysts. God has always used a human instrument as the agent for solidarity and mutuality.

Readers will allow me to mention as one outstanding representative Dr. Randolph Nugent. The general secretary paid visits to the area of Central and Southern Europe and with great empathy listened and responded to our needs. He has initiated and assisted in the development of a structure of awareness in GBGM. He has supported bilateral initiatives like the international consultations. He himself participated as Bible study leader. The Board, which was formerly the "Board in New York," has become "our Board" as we talk about it today.

In the name of the Central Conference of Central and Southern Europe and for the sake of the many whom I should have mentioned here, we express our gratitude and deep appreciation to Dr. Randolph Nugent as a living symbol of the Methodist culture of mutuality. The adjectives I could add to this high qualification would be open, sensitive, prayerful, connected, committed, and responsive.

CHAPTER 8

Visions Shaping the Future
Arturo Fernandez (1993–2000)

*B*EFORE I BECAME a director of the General Board of Global Ministries (GBGM), I served on the General Advance Committee of the church. We met in Brazil one year and visited several projects supported with Advance funds. There I had one of those encounters that was a transforming experience for me.

A couple of us went to a very poor community. Countless children were playing in the streets. Some came to talk with us as we walked through the neighborhood. They came running and jumping with boundless energy and endless smiles on their faces. We talked and shared candy, and we took Polaroid photos to give to them.

We left with a certain exuberance because of the joy given off by these children. We responded with a certain disbelief, then, when our host told us later that these children had little if any meaningful future. These were beautiful children—smiling, loving, friendly. How could they not have a future like our own children and grandchildren?

As we pondered this reality, we kept thinking of the smiles and the apparent joy with which they related to us. Why were these children able to smile so freely in the midst of such cruel poverty and despair? Would I and my own children or grandchildren be able to form the jubilant and inviting gestures that reached so deeply into our hearts?

I believe the whole mission of God in the world is predicated on our ability to believe enough in a meaningful and purposeful future for human existence. God believes in us! God depends on our ability to carry the mission to fruition.

The work of mission is about helping people of all ages and sexes to recover, claim, and experience the Spirit of God that enables them to envision a world in which justice is measured by the spirit and righteousness of God. In this vision, peace and love are the norm of human existence and relationships. Ministries with children and women are basic to the mission work of the church, because often the dreams and visions of children and women are excluded from the mission agenda of the church. Youth also play an essential role in the mission of the church because they have the freedom and ability to dream and have visions that challenge a church often settled and comfortable in old ways of interpreting and living the faith.

When I became a director of GBGM, then, I was glad to see that these ministries with women, children, and youth were an integral part of the mission of The United Methodist Church (UMC). These ministries are the priority for the Women's Division, and through the leadership of United Methodist Women (UMW) they have been integrated into mission throughout the world.

Surpassing Expectations

Yet when I was elected a director and began to serve in the 1993–1996 quadrennium, I was surprised at the extensive and complex mission of the church. At that time the Board comprised 180 members! I was then a district superintendent in the Oregon-Idaho Annual Conference and was elected as an additional member of the Board from the Western Jurisdiction. During that first quadrennium I served as chair of the Latin American/Caribbean Region of the World Program Division. At that time the division had staff teams for global regions. I also served on the Board Hispanic Task Force and became its chair. I had numerous other responsibilities, major ones being the National Plan for Hispanic Ministry Committee and the Mission Evangelism Committee. These experiences gave me a view of many important programs, and since all directors belong to the Board plenary, we had the responsibility of overseeing policy in all areas, including approving the budget.

As I assess my experience over the past eight years, I would say that perhaps our greatest accomplishment was the Russia Initiative. This initiative was not only timely in a historical sense, but it also pushed us into new forms of mission. It was a precursor of the partnership of churches approach that took place in the restructure of the Board later. The Russian initiative was a new venture and was a result of great vision on the part of Dr. Randolph Nugent, the general secretary of the Board, and other Board leaders.

The Russia Initiative enabled us to practice what we were later going to say was the "facilitating" of mission. That is, instead of the Board managing mission, or controlling it, we were going to enable mission among the churches globally. This Russian experience was invaluable as we entered other arenas, Cambodia, for example, and also Venezuela and Honduras, where the initiative actually came from the people themselves, rather than from us. Missioners of Hope is another example. This initiative enables Africans to become missionaries on their own continent. They are moving us away from the traditional ways and moving toward a new way of engagement.

Related to the Russia initiative, and also of great importance, was the ministry in Kazakhstan. There you had a tragedy in which nuclear radiation had affected a large part of the population, and yet in the wake of the changes taking place as the former Soviet Union dissolved, no one was doing anything to help these people. The Board was able to relate United Methodist health institutions in this country to the needs there so that they received the equipment and resources to minister to people who had been exposed to radiation.

Restructuring the Board

Of almost equal importance, however, was the restructuring of the Board, which meant:

1. Reducing the number of directors from 180 to 90;
2. Requiring new ways of thinking on the part of the staff and reorienting, retraining, and reassigning them;
3. Realigning program units to implement new mission directions and a new philosophy of mission;
4. Integrating new understandings brought about by globalization and embracing the concept of a truly global church;
5. Planning, providing funds, and implementing new initiatives in response to global needs and pressure from different constituencies to use unrealized funds;
6. Fulfilling the Board's policy-making responsibilities within this new structure.

Years from now this restructure will be seen as the bold new step that was needed to make The UMC a global church with an invigorated and faithful understanding of mission and ministry required by the new global context. The global context is complex, and it is difficult for an institutional church like ours to remake itself in a way that addresses specifics of that complex. It will be years before we truly restructure. Restructure is not just of organization; it involves attitudes, orientations, assumptions, perspectives.

Perhaps this change cannot be seen as profound because in its early stages it is fraught with internal problems. One of the pains I have felt was that in the first quadrennium I was chair of the Latin American/Caribbean section, where I knew staff was connected to the places and people where mission was being carried out. In the new structure we lost that in going to crossfunctional teams. Apparently we are now moving toward a regional presence in Africa, which indicates that we may have realized that not everything we had in the previous structure was bad.

We are also searching for better ways to relate to the autonomous churches.[1] We have much to learn from them. GBGM cannot be the center of mission for them. The restructure was the first step in redefining our relation to these autonomous churches. My hope is that GBGM will be successful in truly engaging the annual conferences and the ethnic churches. We have *supported* African-American, Asian-American, Hispanic, and Native American churches, but we need to relate to them differently in the future.

In the National Hispanic Plan we have been able to work together in new ways. We have moved beyond thinking that Hispanic mission belongs exclusively to the Hispanic churches. We have incorporated this mission in the total church, and an example is the way non-Hispanic churches are reaching out to Hispanics. We can make the mission with ethnic churches more a part of the whole church in the same way, and the restructuring helps us accomplish this.

Learning to Be Partners

A large part of this new approach to mission is helping annual conferences to understand mission from the perspective of the whole church. I had some experience with this when I was a pastor in the California-Nevada Annual Conference. I was the conference coordinator of Hispanic ministries. We entered into a covenant with the Methodist Church in Bolivia, the Iglesia Evangelica Metodista Boliviana, which was probably the first formal covenant relationship between a UMC annual conference and an autonomous Methodist church.

We brought both parties to the relationship, rather than developing it in the annual conference and then inviting the autonomous church. We took a lot of time to hear what their priorities were and then to move to accountability, asking: At what point are we responsible for calling each other to account? Criticism must be made in light of the greater mission. This was a partner relation with Bolivia, but it also involved GBGM. This is the kind of involvement that means the priority of the annual conference is not exclusive but coordinated. It works as long as GBGM does not have to control everything or act as if it knows everything!

Full participation of partners is a way of countering the issue of control. Some of the churches have complained about control, which they experience as part of the larger, corporate control in their countries. Assurance that we in the U.S. church are not trying to control other churches can come only by a true partner relationship.

Appreciating the Context

What is already beginning to happen between Board mission engagement and annual conference and local church mission will make the purposes of the Board restructure come closer to reality. We must continue to build trust. The annual conference dialogues have been very important. Anything we can do to build bridges of understanding between the Board and the rest of the church will help.

This is true of the global church as well. It is true of the relationships we must continue to build with ethnic constituencies of the church. As we become a global church, to a great extent the ethnic churches are themselves caught in the Christianity of institutional ministry, which tends to be too self-focused. Ethnic groups are focused on their own groups. If we emphasize our uniqueness too much, it will keep us from having a global perspective on mission. The ethnic churches need to relate to the global church as well. There are some beginnings in this area. The Latin American and Caribbean Methodist Council of Churches (Consejo de Iglesias Evangélicas Metodistas en América Latin y el Caribe, or CIEMAL) is a member of the executive committee of the Hispanic caucus in the U.S.

(Metodistas Asociados Representado la Causa de los Hispano-Americanos, or MARCHA), and vice versa. To the extent ethnics in this country can begin to relate beyond their immediate interests, it coincides with the facilitating approach of the Board. We will be engaging in a collaborative way.

Context enables us to see the whole. Context is not a program but a process. The contextual issues include language—I don't mean whether we speak English or Spanish, but the language we use to describe reality. For example, each year I take at least one group to Bolivia and then to Peru, and my concern is to help them to begin to understand their attachment to their own reality and to begin a process of detachment from their own reality, to begin to absorb some of the other reality. Even after training, we still speak our language, our orientation, our concepts. We are driven by discomfort, guilt, and superiority, and we tend to impose these realities, or at least to interpret from that perspective.

Another issue is simply the reality of a different way of life, the reality of a people who live in poverty and the values they hold to, which are very different from ours. Related to that is the marketing of society and the values being imposed on us. Even in the U.S., we tend to be formal or institutional Christians, but the values that really carry us are the values of the marketplace. What is "good" is what is given to us, usually a form of commerce.

This orientation is rapidly flowing into the rest of the world and is bringing tremendous confusion to people who are being asked to be consumers and to respond to values that appeal to the consumer. There is a lot of brokenness in the developing countries because of this. The churches themselves are struggling to interpret to the people what is happening to them.

Context then means understanding language in this sense. We need to rise above each other's predicament and see the larger human predicament. Achieving this perspective takes a lot of thinking, sharing, and experiencing. I call it "encounter." I say we are going for an encounter with Christ in the Americas. If we can't see Christ in the situation we are fixed on people only. Before we go, Christ is at work in those lives. Our task is to discern God working through the least of the people.

The world is experiencing radical changes. Their effect is compounded by the speed at which they are happening. So-called neoliberalism, globalization, and the market economy all depend on mass consumption and cheap labor. The intrusions of massive advertising of products and the inculcation of materialistic values are destructive of traditional communities and their cultures. One of the great challenges facing us in the church is how we are to proclaim the gospel of Jesus Christ in a world so culturally and religiously diverse. Traditional values have been replaced by consumer propaganda hawked to us day and night by what Harvey Cox calls market missionaries who believe they have the answer.[2] The church must consider all these factors as it plans its mission into the twenty-first century.

Planning Mission

As chair of the Mission Development Committee of the Board in this quadrennium, I presided over the discussions and decisions on all the mission initiatives during that time. This committee reviews all the major recommendations for programs and initiatives that come before the Board. The committee recommends actions to the plenary and when it acts it becomes the actual mission of the church. The Board has a comprehensive plan for mission, a document that takes into account the context for mission. It also sets goals and describes strategies the various units of the Board have for reaching those goals.

One initiative that came out of this process in the last four years was the Millennium Fund for Mission. As a result of a favorable stock market, the Board benefitted from additional amounts of money that could be used for mission. The Millennium Fund was a major breakthrough in showing how the Board and the church could respond to a new situation. The money was used to help rebuild churches in Africa destroyed or damaged during their recent civil wars, to purchase property and build new churches in eastern Europe, and to meet the urgent problems facing urban ministries in the U.S. The process was also new: the Board asked annual conferences to provide matching funds, thus increasing the amounts that could be used and illustrating how the Board could be partners in mission with the annual conferences.

There were additional amounts of money available to the Board during the quadrennium. This money proved to be both a blessing and a curse. In some ways we were being pressured to use the money and we may have made decisions prematurely. We have done good things, but how is a good thing measured? We were not ready as a Board structurally to engage in the types of ministries we initiated. We have not been able to spend quality time to go through all the processes of restructuring, particularly the attitudes, understandings, new languages, relations between partners, and healing among the people who are affected by the restructure.

The Millennium Fund also omitted Asia and Latin America. In order to correct this omission, I and others developed the Partnership Fund for Latin America. It is aimed at new mission opportunities emerging in Latin America and the Caribbean and in Asia, regions not covered by the Millennium Fund. Priority will be given to innovative programs with mission partners that show promise of generating ongoing support, both locally and globally. Major emphases will include leadership development, training in evangelization and community ministries, and the use of electronic media. These are examples of how we can empower churches in places like Latin America. This is what we hope annual conferences will do, also, so that the churches in Latin America and other places will not simply be looking for us to provide money continually for projects but be able to develop themselves.

We still have a long way to go in learning from this situation, because after the market stops producing these high returns and we are back with a limited budget, what have we learned?

One change we need to make is to incorporate some of the learnings from all our consultations into the program of the Board. These meetings with people from the annual conferences, central conferences, and autonomous churches are rich and loaded with insights. We don't always integrate them very well into the ongoing work of mission, however, which is something that could be included in the planning process.

Interpreting Mission

My coming from the Rio Grande Conference as a converted Roman Catholic has created a certain passion for what the gospel can do in one's life. It has made me realize the transformation that can occur and the social context of that conversion experience. Because of this I have always had a passion for mission. My role in coming to GBGM was natural for me and a continuation of my role in the church. My various assignments have always been roles of teaching mission. That was the purpose of my taking these groups to Latin America.

Interpreting is an integral part of being a director. It enables one to clarify misunderstandings that may occur in one's annual conference. No director should "defend" the Board. To be a United Methodist is to be critical! We're not yes people. But if you are on this Board there is no way you can deny the great work the Board does.

Changing Mission in the New Millennium

We will have to do things differently in the future. A U.S. board like GBGM will no longer be the center from which missionaries are sent into the world. Electronic communications like the internet will continue to enhance direct communications between local churches and their sister churches throughout the world. Missionaries will include a majority of laity, including many professionals, who will do short- and long-term assignments. GBGM will implement mission based on needs discovered by laity in mission. We will have to take account of the Pentecostal revival that is bringing hope to millions who live on the periphery of power and wealth. Harvey Cox believes our "text-oriented" denominations often dismiss Pentecostals as irrelevant fanatics.

Having said this let me also say that an institutional form of Christianity like ours will always need the general agencies of the church or their replacements. I believe the focus in the future will center on equipping and resourcing the laity for ministry and mission. This will be done through partnerships with annual conferences and through multimedia resources and electronic media. The more The UMC becomes a global entity, the more important will become the role of agencies as enablers, facilitators, and bridges of communication.

Being in Community

About four years ago a former Presbyterian minister was with us when we went to Bolivia and Peru. We always debrief the experience, have dialogue, and exchange reflections, so that we learn from each other. During the debriefing this minister, who is now a UMC layman, said, "I was trained as a minister. I went to seminary and studied the Bible. I thought I understood the Bible and the meaning of Christianity. I thought I knew who Christ was. But it was not until I came here to Bolivia that I encountered Christ in the lives of these people, and I have come to know who the living Christ is." With tears he shared this transformation with us.

Christ is not in the clouds. Christ is already among us. Our spirit must be prepared to discern his presence, and we cannot do this alone; we must do it in community.

Now that I concluded eight years as a director in GBGM, I must say a word about its community of directors and staff. My understanding and appreciation of mission at all levels of the church and global settings have been enriched through the lives and actions of directors and staff. The directors and the staff who have served in the Mission Development Committee during the 1992–2000 quadrennia are a great example of the dedication, wisdom, and courage that is required for global mission in a complex and conflicted world. I have been privileged to learn from the staff, particularly those with whom I have had close association in my various roles on the Board.

Michael Rivas, the deputy general secretary for planning and research, is a friend whose comprehensive knowledge of mission and the structure of GBGM has provided the needed support and guidance for the Mission Development Committee. S T Kimbrough, associate general secretary for mission evangelism, has helped us in our struggles to articulate and express mission in word and song in the light of our rich Wesleyan heritage. David Wu and Sharon Maeda have brought new perspectives and gifts to the way we do mission. Lorene F. Wilbur, deputy secretary for administration, brings the strength of administrative detail and gracious personality to the institutional life of GBGM. Robert Harman, deputy general secretary, is one from whom I have learned much about mission in the global context. Bob's vision and theological understanding of mission will continue to inform the work of mission in GBGM for years beyond his retirement. The ministry of United Methodist Committee on Relief (UMCOR) in the world is one of the most exciting and meaningful engagements of mission in the global context. This quadrennium has witnessed some far-reaching initiatives through UMCOR under the innovative and perceptive leadership of its deputy general secretary, Paul Dirdak. The Reverend Kinmoth (Kim) Jefferson, now deceased, was a staff person responsible for urban ministries and one with whom I was associated since the early 1970s. Kim was an invaluable consultant in the work of the Mission Development Committee. My appreciation for the Women's Division role in the life and ministry of GBGM has always been high, but the past few years have given me a broader understanding of its importance in the larger context of the church. The courageous witness of United Methodist Women in the sensitive areas of mission will continue to carry us into the twenty-first

Two girls cross a bridge in San Isidro, Honduras, built by villagers after Hurricane Mitch ravaged their country in 1998. The bridge was built with assistance from the Christian Commission for Development (CCD), a Honduran church group. CCD is a member of Action by Churches Together, an international alliance of church relief agencies that includes the United Methodist Committee on Relief. *(Photo by Paul Jeffrey, United Methodist New Service)*

century! Joyce D. Sohl's strong leadership and insightful mind as deputy general secretary of the Women's Division are evidence of the many gifts of the GBGM staff.

There are many others in the professional staff and the support staff who could be mentioned. They are a committed group bringing a wide range of skills and gifts to the ministry and mission of GBGM.

Our general secretary, Dr. Randolph Nugent, is a person with great discernment and insight about past and contemporary social and political movements. His vision and capacity to lead in innovative ways that respond to the nuances of the emerging so-called paradigms for understanding present reality have been demonstrated by the many initiatives that have been implemented under his leadership. It is hard for me to imagine how one person can survive, carrying the massive weight of GBGM on his shoulders, as Randy has done all these years. I think an important part of the reason lies in the commitment and dedication of the professional and support staff.

There is no way I can describe the sheer joy and hope that I experience at each gathering of GBGM. It may be through the moving, challenging, penetrating words spoken in worship. It may be in the plenaries, hearing reports on the many mission initiatives. It may be in the units of the Board, sitting next to Christians of the world on the right and on the left, discussing or describing the mission of God in particular settings. It may be in the commissioning service for new missionaries.

Indeed, we are a Pentecostal community of colorful vintage and of many languages. Even if each of us were to speak in our own language, our hearts would understand the love conveyed!

CHAPTER 9

Witnessing to the Gospel in Word and Deed
Jenni Yeoh (1993–2000)

"'Go therefore and make disciples of all nations, baptizing them in the name of the Father and of the Son and of the Holy Spirit, and teaching them to obey everything that I have commanded you. And remember, I am with you always, to the end of the age.'" (New Revised Standard Version)

The faithful response of the General Board of Global Ministries (GBGM) to this Scripture, Matthew 28:19–20, changed my life. Missionaries were sent all over the world to bring the gift of the gospel of Jesus Christ. I am one of the recipients of this gift. Perhaps because I am a product of mission, I have been proud to serve as the director of GBGM. This is a Board that preaches the gospel in word and deed.

I grew up in a Buddhist home in western Malaysia. My father died when I was very young, and my mom raised me and provided my education in one of the best private schools in the country, Holly Methodist School, which was built by The United Methodist Church (UMC) and is in Telok Anson, Malaysia. In my last year of high school I met Donald Small, a United Methodist missionary who changed my life. He taught and witnessed to me the love of Jesus Christ. I was baptized and joined the Methodist Church of Malaysia. Later I married a Methodist clergyman. I went on to teach in a Methodist school. I was also a volunteer counselor for a girls' hostel, Shellabear Hall in Malacca, built and owned by the Women's Division. In 1973 our family came to the U.S., where my husband received a scholarship to Southern Methodist University. He received his doctorate there. In thanksgiving for all that God has provided, I have committed my life to serve Jesus Christ. Praise be to God!

Taking an Initiative for Health

As a layperson active in my local church and annual conference, and as a woman trained by United Methodist Women (UMW), I was quite knowledgeable about The UMC and its commitment to mission before being elected a director in 1992. UMW provides job training for all officers. UMW also provides many opportunities to ethnic women. It has truthfully been said that UMW takes an ordinary woman and makes her extraordinary.

Even so, I was awed by the human need and the many services offered by GBGM on becoming a director. In the first quadrennium, when I was elected by the Western Jurisdiction, I was vice chair of the Mission Evangelism Committee, and we made a great contribution by working with Associate General Secretary S T Kimbrough to produce the songbook, *Global Praise*. This songbook consists of songs from our Christian brothers and sisters from around the globe and has been used in our Global Gatherings and also at the Pacific Northwest Gathering modeled after the one sponsored by the Board. The songbook has since been used at many United Methodist and UMW events.

In the second quadrennium, I was one of thirty UM women across the church elected to serve on the Board. During this quadrennium I have been a member of Health and Relief, which comprises both the United Methodist Committee on Relief (UMCOR) and Health and Welfare Ministries. UMCOR is one of the most important units of the Board. Its "three Rs" are response (to disaster), relief, and rebuilding. It rebuilds not only structures but communities and lives. I had the opportunity to work at the UMCOR depot in Louisiana. I did not realize how large it is until I got there. The Medicine Boxes and other supplies, such as health kits, education kits, flood buckets, and water pumps, are all sent with love by UM churches. A couple of years ago, GBGM directors were asked to make a commitment to provide one Medicine Box from each of their local churches. My church was so excited it sent three boxes.[1]

But the most significant initiative I was involved in as a director was serving on the Kendall Fund Committee. During this second quadrennium I had the privilege of serving as chair of the committee that administered the fund. The Kendall Fund is the only fund in the history of GBGM that has designated its grants to African Americans and poor whites. The fund originated with Harry R. Kendall, who was born and

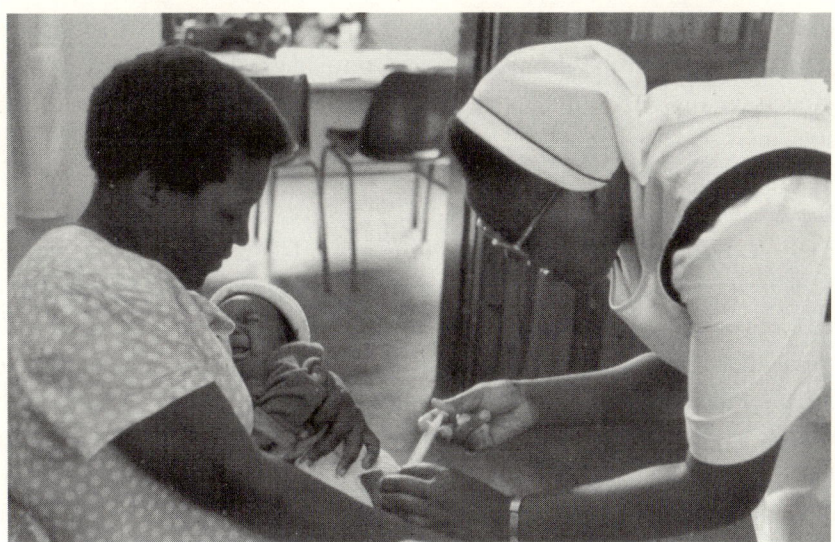

A health care worker gives a baby a DPTP booster shot [diptheria-tetanus-pertussis (whooping cough)-polio] in Lisutu, Zambia, during a famine in 2002. United Methodists worked to provide food and health services through the ecumenical coalition of Action by Churches Together (ACT), with contributions through the Africa Famine Relief advance program of the United Methodist Committee on Relief. *(Photo by Richard Lord, UMCOR © 2002)*

raised on a farm in Kentucky. As a boy he was poor, worked in the fields, and got his first job currying and harnessing stagecoach horses. At age seventeen he became an agent for the Prudential Insurance Company and from there went on to become chairman of the board of Washington National, another insurance company. He held that position until his death in 1958.

He never forgot his roots and on his death he left the bulk of his estate to a trust fund whose beneficiaries were charitable, religious, and educational institutions. He wanted his assets to provide direct services and educational opportunities to the disadvantaged and marginalized, particularly African Americans. The Methodist Board of Hospitals and Homes and its successors, down to the present Health and Welfare Ministries, received investment income from part of this fund until the corpus was dissolved and distributed in 1998. During those forty years the Methodist and United Methodist churches provided grants to benefit African

Americans and poor whites as Mr. Kendall designated. GBGM received a large amount from the distribution and was able to finance many needed projects in 1998 and 1999. The funds grew because of increases in the stock market.

An exciting thing happened at the 2000 spring Board meeting: an amount of $8 million from this fund was granted for the construction of a Harry R. Kendall Science and Health Mission Center at Philander Smith College in Little Rock, Arkansas. Appropriately, the Mission Center component will be named after Dr. Randolph Nugent.

Philander Smith is one of the African-American colleges related to The UMC, and it has many students from the Arkansas Delta, one of the poorest economic regions of the country. The health science students at the college have a 90 percent acceptance rate at medical schools, however. Some of these students grew up in families so poor the students had never seen a doctor until they entered college. The Harry R. Kendall Science and Health Mission Center will fulfill Mr. Kendall's vision by providing opportunities for direct services as well as leadership development. The mission of the center is to develop students with skills in critical thinking, intellectual curiosity, and a desire for lifelong learning, which will lead to preparation for successful placement. Through the programs of the center, the college will work with GBGM in congregational health ministries and community-based primary health care, while also teaming up with Meharry Medical College in Nashville, Tennessee, to educate primary care physicians. Meharry is also one of the African-American schools related to The UMC.

The fund also provided a $1.5 million matching grant to Gulfside Assembly to build a new facility to provide spiritual and medical training to the African-American community. Another grant was to a community center for a phone system, which seems small but meets a real need. Other grants have gone for housing for the poor and apartments for the aging. Some scholarships are granted to nurses and others preparing for careers in health care. More than $3 million was disbursed for these grants in 2001. The Board will continue to make grants from the returns on the funds.[2]

Continuing the Board but Changing the Mission

The Board is the conduit in which mission is done. The Board does mission for what the local church cannot do on its own. One church cannot build an Africa University or support a health sciences center that helps to meet the huge need for more African-American doctors in this country. UM churches can do it together.

I have certainly learned the value of the Board. The Board transforms, restores hope, and provides educational skills so people can be independent. Here I learned to work with people of faith who have made a commitment to Jesus Christ. They lived up to the mission that Jesus set forth in Luke 4:16–19. This is a Board that listens, prays, and works together. The role of this agency is to make disciples, to feed the hungry, and to meet the needs of God's people.

Having said that, I also believe that our work will change in the future. Because the context of mission is constantly changing, we will need to do mission in a new way in the future

One of the changes is that we need to be invited to do mission. We have learned this in UMCOR, where we make a response when we are asked to. For years Malaysia has received missionaries from America, which has been wonderful. We have learned to train people to be their own missionaries, however. In Malaysia it is illegal to proselyte Muslims. We have to respect those laws. Years ago it was a free-for-all, and you could go where you wanted. Nowadays we are more sensitive to the needs of the people of those countries and go where we are invited. Moreover, we have educated many people who returned to their own countries to provide needed services. Years ago we had to sing only Western tunes, but now we sing Malaysian tunes to words from the Scripture. We have learned to respect people's culture and hope that God speaks through their culture.

Being Grateful

It has been a joy to work with a staff that is knowledgeable, resourceful, and professional. This is a committed staff—not just committed, *very* committed. I am grateful for the opportunity to serve. It has helped me grow as a Christian. It has helped me open my mind. It has helped me see the world from a wider perspective and to be more sensitive to the needs of others. As an ethnic it has helped me to be sensitive to *other* ethnics. We are from different cultures. We learn from the different people with whom we minister, God's people with different religious and cultural backgrounds.

I am especially grateful for the opportunity to work with General Secretary Dr. Randolph Nugent. He is a brilliant man and very resourceful.

Ask him anything and he will give you the information on the ministries you want to know about. He is also very encouraging with people. Dr. Nugent represents the Board very well. He is very passionate about mission, and it shows in his work, his speech, and his personality.

I have indeed been blessed and am grateful for the opportunity to serve on GBGM.

CHAPTER 10

Fifty Years after the Universal Declaration of Human Rights:
A Latin American and Caribbean Perspective
Frederico J. Pagura (1998)

(This article is based on an address in 1998 to the Eighth General Assembly of the World Council of Churches in Harare, Zimbabwe. The author was Methodist bishop in Central America 1969–1973 and now lives in Argentina. The article was translated by Nilda Ferrari and is published here with permission of the author. Although not a director of the General Board of Global Ministries, he has been a frequent visitor and consultant to it. Ed.)

DEAR SISTERS AND BROTHERS in the faith, hope and love given to us by God "through the resurrection of Jesus Christ" (I Peter 1:3, New Revised Standard Version):

I am grateful to the World Council of Churches for giving us the opportunity to make our voices and our testimony heard, from the very heart of our dark-skinned America, on the occasion of this, the fiftieth anniversary of the Universal Declaration of Human Rights. And I will begin by invoking one of the few rights still left to the elderly on our American continent, that is, to try to remember, to recall, in my case, an ecumenical leader who was well-recognized in his time, Dr. Charles Malik of Beirut. He presided over the United Nations General Assembly for the approval of the declaration we commemorate today. In 1971, he also presided over the final Assembly of the World Council of Christian Education in Huampaní, Peru. There I had to read the lecture "New Theological Perspectives from Latin America" of Dr. Míguez Bonino in his absence. I was showered with criticism, particularly by theologians and leaders of the First World, because at that time Liberation Theology was being born, along with the writings of Rubén Alves of Brazil and Gustavo Gutiérrez of Peru, in a bold effort simultaneously to listen to and connect (in the words of our censored martyr, Bishop Enrique Angelelli of Argentina) "the voice of the gospel and the cry of our people."[1]

Considering Obstacles to Human Rights

What has happened between that time and now in our Latin American and Caribbean countries, from an evangelical and ecumenical perspective? On the one hand, innumerable efforts have been made to translate the cold words of the Universal Declaration into the burning reality of the lives of our people. And in this regard we recognize and give thanks for the extraordinary contribution of the World Council of Churches. But at the same time we have stumbled upon the obstacle of the political-economic-military complex which predominates in our world, such that the advances achieved at times in various regions and which were inspired by this fundamental document, are suddenly obliterated (in the past by military coups; and now by arbitrary blockades or invasions of entire nations, destructive economic-financial blows, unbearable pressures, etc.), an experience familiar to us in these times.

In an article entitled "Asignaturas Pendientes" ("An Unfinished Agenda") in a magazine with a vast continental circulation, Alberto Giudice described the situation:

> Today, in the final decade of the century, human rights violations mean specifically: torture, the rape and sexual mutilation of women, children traumatized in their development (prostituted or subjected to shameful conditions of slave labor), and human beings who seek refuge far from their homelands for economic, political or religious reasons. Persons traumatized by these horrible occurrences have great difficulty, despite the help they may receive, integrating normally into society.

Even more drastically, Dr. Alejandro Teitelbaum, permanent representative in Geneva of the American Association of Lawyers, affirms: "The international system of human rights, built on the 'Universal Declaration' is failing and is being replaced by the Declaration of the Rights of Transnationals, through the Multilateral Agreement on Investments. Someone has said that the right of nations to govern themselves is being replaced by the right of transnationals to govern nations."[2]

The grandmothers (*abuelas*) of Argentina protested during that country's military dictatorship that the government was not giving them information on their loved ones who had "disappeared." Their courageous protests at the Plaza de Mayo plaza in Buenos Aires kept pressure on the government before the world. *(Photo by Lyssette Perez-Salgado)*

Significantly, in the darkest times of military dictatorships, the Uruguayan theologian Juan Luis Segundo had already denounced it: "The powers of the North who are appalled at the terrible Human Rights violations in Latin America and the Caribbean are the same ones who make the true exercise of democracy in our countries practically impossible." (An accusation clearly illustrated in the film *Missing*, ever-current in its significance, and emphasized by the anxiously sought trial of General August Pinochet and other genocidal military leaders, which we are celebrating today throughout Latin America and the Caribbean and throughout the world, as a milestone in the broad and difficult struggle against impunity and for truth and justice.)

The second Latin American meeting of bishops and pastors of the Consejo Latinoamericano de Iglesias (CLAI) on "Foreign Debt and Narcotrafficking," which took place in 1990 in Kingston, Jamaica, had already led us to declare: "We have approached the issues of the meeting conscious of the confrontation between two forms of logic: the logic of capital that puts money before human beings as the new idol that demands human lives and blood; and the logic of a life inspired by the Gospel, which places a supreme value on the human being, and leads us to respect Nature and to seek an alternative economic order which would guarantee decent living conditions."[3]

Thus we understand why the report, "Justicia, Paz y Creación" ("Justice, Peace and Creation"), in the Section on International Matters of CLAI states: "One characteristic of this period has been the intertwining of the concerns for human rights, peace, conflict resolution, questions regarding armaments, and world government."[4]

For us, human rights (including the inevitable issues of impunity, foreign debt and exclusion, freedom of the press and information, disarmament and arms trafficking, violence, peace, world government, and the United Nations) constitute an indivisible reality and an urgent imperative in the battle for life to which we have been committed, and in which our ecumenical council has a legacy and a prophetic role which we cannot renounce or weaken at this critical time, at the risk of losing our call to action.

Seeking Truth, Justice, and Peace

I would like to conclude with three references that are directly related to our firm commitment as seekers of truth, justice, and peace. The first sprang from the lips of South African President Nelson Mandela, addressing his colleagues from Mercosur (an economic agreement among the countries of the southern region of South America), whom he visited in a Patagonian city in Argentina about the middle of 1999. He said there: "If there is no food when people are hungry, if there is no medicine when they are sick, if there is ignorance, and the basic rights of people are not respected, then democracy is an empty shell, even if the citizens vote and have parliaments."[5]

The second one comes to us from one of the true prophets who represent the source of the spiritual and moral thinking of our America, the Brazilian theologian, Leonardo Boff. In an interview he gave in Mexico, he said: "As part of the rights of the poor against poverty and in favor of life, consideration must be given to the earth as the most impoverished among the poor. Because without the earth, without the biosphere we cannot guarantee any other project." Therefore he adds that today ecology is the basis of another essential question: "The great question is not, what is the future of the Church, but rather, what is the future of the earth, what is the future of humanity, and in what way can the Church help to guarantee that future."[6]

The third resounded unanimously at the second meeting of bishops and pastors in Kingston, Jamaica: "Today faith requires personal conversion and commitment to structural change. Without personal conversion structural change will lead to new forms of oppression and alienation of the human being. Without commitment to structural change, conversion disappears into a self-absorbed, individualistic and detached spirituality."[7]

May God guide and sustain us so that we will not be "rebels against the celestial vision" offered to us by this new millennium and this time of celebration.

CHAPTER 11

Mission: A Commitment to Action
Joel Martinez (2000–2002)

*T*HE GENERAL BOARD of Global Ministries (GBGM) seeks to be faithful to God's mission throughout the world. This mission is rooted in The United Methodist Church (UMC) outreach across all the boundaries that divide the human family. It is theologically centered in witness to God's self-giving love in Jesus Christ. God's action in Christ is summarized in the Gospel of John: "And the word became flesh and lived among us . . . " (1:14, NRSV). This affirmation defines, inspires, and motivates the Board's witness and service.

This report on the Board from late 2000 into 2002 is an appropriate reminder of the church's call to embody the gospel in grace-inspired deeds. In commending this report to readers, I propose four characteristics of our missional commitment to action: that it is daring in scope, inclusive in outreach, open to the gifts of all, and expressed in partnerships for the full gospel.[1]

Daring in Scope

The scope of the global ministries entrusted to the Board is mind- and heart-stretching. The widest horizons of human need are the ordinary boundaries of Christian mission. The vision of the Board is not confined to neat boundaries defined by fixed duties. The cries of humanity must be heard, regardless of the location, station, class, or color of the suffering ones. Hearing and responding become daring and often daunting responsibilities. The resources may be insufficient, the services limited, and the capacity inadequate, but the expectations raised by the voices remain high. Indeed, past responses breed higher expectations for the future. It is a tide of rising expectations for services that presents a major challenge to the Board in the early twenty-first century.

Are we, as United Methodists, up to the challenge of embracing the world in all its pain and poverty, its sin and separation, its disparity and delusions? We say "yes" through the General Board of Global Ministries.

Response to Events of September 11

This willingness to embrace the world in its pain was most evident in 2001 in the church's response to the tragedies of September 11. When airliners flown by terrorists struck targets in New York City and Washington, D.C., with another hijacked plane going down in Pennsylvania, the people of God responded. The United Methodist Committee on Relief (UMCOR), United Methodist Volunteers in Mission, and members of the New York Conference ministered tirelessly at Ground Zero. United Methodist chaplains comforted grieving families at the Pentagon.

Health and Relief

UMCOR responded to the events of September 11 by providing immediate and ongoing trauma counseling, supporting peacemaking activities between Arab and non-Arab groups in various parts of the U.S., and assisting immigrants who were affected. As part of its "Love in the Midst of Tragedy" response, UMCOR also helped the people of Afghanistan by supplying tents, household and kitchen items, and food and by supporting a quilt-making project that enables refugee women to earn income.

UMCOR also fulfilled its calling to help people directly in need in many other ways during 2000–2002. In 2000, UMCOR Refugee Ministries helped to resettle 440 families, or a total of 1,360 people, in the U.S. They came from 24 countries. In 2001, UMCOR helped resettle 328 families, or 886 people, from 15 countries. In both years some 150 United Methodist congregations assisted in resettling these families through sponsorship, and a number of congregations provided donations for arriving refugees. The decrease in arriving refugees in 2001 was a direct result of a U.S. Government decision virtually halting refugee arrivals and resettlement following the events of September 11.

UMCOR also worked with United Methodists in war-torn Liberia to open a school in Gbason and revitalize a hospital in Ganta. It continued to help the people of Kosovo recover from warfare fueled in part by ethnic tensions. It supported land mine removal in Mozambique using new tech-

Bits of steel structure were all that remained of the World Trade Center complex in lower Manhattan after the terrorist attacks of September 11, 2001. *(Photo by John Goodwin, United Methodist News Service)*

nology that clears mined areas more safely and quickly. It provided emergency relief to famine victims in Africa, Afghanistan, North Korea, and Central America. It assisted Palestinians suffering from renewed violence in the Middle East. It helped victims of Hurricane Floyd in North Carolina and the Bahamas, Hurricane Iris in Belize, Hurricane Michelle in Central America and Cuba, and Tropical Storm Allison in Texas. And it continued to respond to earthquake victims in India, El Salvador, and Turkey. The UMCOR Depot, part of the Sager-Brown facility in Baldwin, Louisiana, processed and shipped 267 tons in 2000 and 222 tons in 2001.

Health and Welfare Ministries held training programs in Africa, Asia, and Latin America in 2000 on Comprehensive Community-based Primary Health Care (CCPHC). In 2001, in addition to the regular CCPHC events, special sessions for prosthesis technicians were held. The Medicine Box program enabled almost 2,220 boxes to be shipped to thirty-five countries in 2000. Each of these boxes provides essential drugs and medical supplies for one thousand people for three months.

Community Ministries

Several worthwhile initiatives were undertaken, beginning with Communities of Shalom, which now constitute a network of transformational ministries in 450 locations. Communities of Shalom in 2000–2002 formed new international partnerships in Zimbabwe and Ghana with the Baltimore-Washington and Texas annual conferences, respectively.

Ministries with Women, Children, and Families responded vigorously to needs created by welfare reform in the U.S. In collaboration with the Women's Division, seventy-six grants were made to UM and ecumenical programs dealing with the crises caused by the welfare-to-work system.

The Special Program on Substance Abuse and Related Violence (SPSARV) sponsored a global conference, Hope of the World, in 2001 that brought together people from twenty-six European and African countries to explore solutions to addiction. The office of Town and Country Ministries worked on a National Plan for Town and Country Ministries, as mandated by General Conference. A series of Holy Boldness Academies provided opportunities for urban clergy and laity to study, reflect, and plan together for ministry in their particular situations.

In addition, the 103 National Mission Institutions comprise community centers, schools and colleges, therapeutic treatment centers, and residences for women across the U.S. These institutions voluntarily participate in a Sharing Partners Action Network, which is a quadrennial initiative to strengthen institutions, train boards of directors, foster shared vision, and reduce financial dependence on the Board, while seeking resources for new services, initiatives, and sites.

Communications

The Board continued the traditional but effective means of print publishing and video production and distribution, but a new initiative was especially noteworthy. Radio Africa International (RAI) began daily shortwave broadcasts on January 1, 2001. Beamed at Africa via a European transmitter in both English and French, the signals reach millions of people. Originally intended as a response to the HIV/AIDS epidemic, RAI also covers other health information, spiritual and religious values, the work of the church in society, economic development, women's issues, environmental themes, and peace and justice concerns. The format includes music, news, drama, and interviews.

Another creative initiative is the development of indigenous resources. To fulfill its commitment in mission education, The UMC is beginning to develop resources that are culturally appropriate for emerging churches in such places as Cambodia, Estonia, Haiti, Lithuania, Latvia, and Senegal. In developing these resources, GBGM is collaborating with the General Board of Discipleship.

Mutuality in Mission: A Theological Principle for the 21st Century, published in 2002, explores both the theology and the operation of Christian mission in the contemporary world. The emphasis is on the dynamics of mission in a global community of many races, nationalities, cultures, and languages. The message is connection and unity. The authors are Glory and Jacob Dharmaraj, United Methodists from India.

Peace in the Congo

The Democratic Republic of the Congo (DRC) is suffering from the effects of four years of civil war. According to *New World Outlook*, "A study by the International Rescue Committee has estimated that approximately 2.5 million Congolese have died from war-related causes. About 85 percent of these deaths were from disease and malnutrition, direct results of the war's destruction of agricultural, economic, health, and infrastructure systems."

President Joseph Kabila has been meeting with dissident groups in an attempt to bring long-term peace and stability to the DRC. As *New World Outlook* reported, "The interfaith community in the DR Congo has also been working to define a plan to ease the country out of its war crisis into a time of peace. In February 2000, the General Board of Global Ministries funded a three-week forum, organized by United Methodist Bishop Onema Fama, of the Central, Northeast, Upper, and West annual conferences in the Congo, to discuss ways to build peace in the country. The forum brought together religious leaders of different faiths." In March 2001, the World Council of Churches brought together agencies of many faith groups to work on implementing peace.

"In June 2001, Dr. Randolph Nugent traveled to the Congo to meet President Joseph Kabila to discuss ways in which The United Methodist Church could assist in the peacebuilding process in the country."[2] Following that meeting, Bishop Onema Fama said that the churches could educate people in the fundamentals of reconciliation and also expose the abuse and terror visited on the Congolese during the conflict. In the meantime, support is still needed for widows and orphans, adult education, training for community-based health programs, moving "child-soldiers" back into society, and AIDS seminars.

Angola Reconstruction

A cease-fire was signed in Angola on April 4, 2002, but much of the country lay in ruins. The toll in land mines alone was staggering, and unexploded land mines still threaten lives. The capital, Luanda, received many displaced people during the conflict, and now they must be resettled or absorbed as workers. The government is now organizing camps for rebel soldiers and their families and providing them with food, shelter, and other basic needs. The United Nations is providing some aid as well.

The United Methodist bishops, José Quipungo and Gaspar Domingos, say that church leaders and members are now free to travel throughout the country to spread the gospel. They are also working to rehabilitate facilities lost during the conflict. Both bishops support the peace process, which includes having a dialogue among the formerly warring factions. The churches are full of people, but Bishop Quipungo said, "Even before the war ended, our numbers were growing. The United Methodist Church strives to be a self-sustaining church, but with so many displaced people now returning with nothing, to nothing, we are in an odd situation. Instead of the members supporting the church, the members expect the church to support them."[3]

The seminary in Negaje, which had to be closed during the conflict, has reopened in Luanda and in 2002 had sixteen professors and forty-five candidates for ministry. Dr. Laurinda Vidal Quipungo, the wife of Bishop Quipungo, is the director of the health department for The UMC in Angola. She is a medical doctor who now works for the state health system. She has built a health post in an outlying area and now has a six-bed facility and three nurses. GBGM has provided medical supplies for Dr. Quipungo. Another large need that GBGM is considering how to help meet is education for children and women. In the rural areas, 50 to 60 percent of women are illiterate.

The UMC is also working with Action by Churches Together (ACT) to rebuild the legal system in Angola. ACT has worked closely with the Human Rights Division of the UN office in Angola to train pastors and church leaders as human rights counselors or peace and reconciliation counselors. Most provinces have no judicial or penal system. A UN survey showed that only thirteen of 164 municipalities had municipal courts that actually functioned. This institutional gap has dire results for the four million Angolans displaced by the war. Not only are there arbitrary beatings and arrests when displaced persons cannot present adequate personal identification, but women and girls are often attacked and even raped by policemen and soldiers as they are collecting water. Soldiers and traditional authorities also demand bribes to put people on lists to obtain assistance. ACT is holding workshops to encourage the displaced to know their rights.

Another large need after the long and bitter war is reconciliation. At an ecumenical service of worship in 2002, local leaders of churches and other community groups were able to talk directly with former combatants in the war. ACT was also involved in a workshop where fifty-nine peace counselors were trained. Police abuse of civilians was a major topic of the workshop. Emilio Cesar, the coordinator for the ACT program on rights, reconciliation, and peace in Moxico province, referred to the former rebels who were now coming into the towns and cities: "With these people emerging from the bush, there cannot be room for revenge or rancor. And the church is in a unique position to help create this culture of peace. The church is a bridge. It's present in every village, and it's willing to get involved without fear."[4]

Inclusive in Outreach

A global agency of the church is not free to pick and choose its areas of service. Although the *Book of Discipline* defines our objectives, we are also commissioned by the biblical mandate: " . . . you will be my witnesses in Jerusalem, in all Judea and Samaria, and to the ends of the earth" (Acts 1:8*b*, NRSV). In seeking to be faithful to this sending order, the Board engages, invites, and includes God's diverse family in its ministries.

Being inclusive in ministry is not easy in a world of increasing conflicts, disparities, and suspicions. Yet, in ways that celebrate and affirm the gospel, the Board consistently demonstrates that racial, ethnic, economic, linguistic, political, and national boundaries are not barriers but meeting places where the miracle of new life in Christ begins. People of all ages and histories are not only served but invited to become servants of others by offering their gifts to the Lord of the church. The Board has a particular charge with regard to the concerns, leadership, and resources of women in mission.

Women's Initiatives

The Women's Division worked with Mission Personnel, a unit of GBGM, in setting up a new category of commissioned missionaries to minister specifically to women, children, and youth. Called "regional missionaries," these women will serve three-year terms in Africa, Asia, or Latin America. Initial mission priorities were identified by women and youth themselves, partly through a series of regional conferences held in the early 1990s. These missionaries are located in Cameroon, Costa Rica, Ghana, Kenya, Nigeria, the Philippines, Senegal, and the U.S.

UMW held its quadrennial assembly in Philadelphia in 2002 under the theme, "Sing a New Song." Nearly 10,000 participants engaged in worship and Bible study, listened to speakers discussing critical issues for women and children, and took part in sixty-three focus groups.

Marion Wright Edelman, the founder and president of the Children's Defense Fund, spoke. Following her speech, participants at the assembly wrote letters to U.S. senators and representatives advocating the reauthorization of the federal Child Care and Development Block Grant and asking for a fund increase over the next five years. Other speakers addressed the effects of violence and war on children, the Israeli-Palestinian conflict, global poverty and racism, and the importance of education in lifting people out of poverty.

United Methodist Women (UMW) continued its drive to involve youth with a National Gathering of Teen and College / University Women held in St. Charles, Illinois, in late 2000. Approximately 800 teens, college and university women, and adult members of UMW participated in Bible study, workshops, worship, plenary sessions and small-group discussions.

Other noteworthy gatherings were a Leadership Development Training and Dialogue for Asian Women at Ewha University in Seoul, Korea; a gathering of fifty women from Latin American churches at the Universal Biblica Latinoamericana in Costa Rica; and the Bible Women's Pilot project follow-up training in Sibu, Sarawak, East Malaysia.

UMW followed up on the crisis created in 1996 by new federal and state welfare policies in the U.S. Fourteen new programs in local churches and mission institutions received grants to assist women and families adversely affected by welfare reform. UMW continued also to provide significant funds for United Methodist mission through $20 million each year in undesignated giving.

Initiatives for Mission   [121]

The faces of these women reflect the spirit of joy and praise that United Methodist Women experienced during the quadrennial Womens' Assembly held in Orlando, Florida, in 1998. *(Photo by Mike DuBose, United Methodist Communications)*

Open to the Gifts of All

The Board invites the gifts of people of all nations and communities into the mission of Christ. While it sends missionaries from the U.S. to other regions, the Board also encourages the use of indigenous missionaries. Throughout Africa, Asia, and Latin America, the Board supports the placement of Persons in Mission among those nearest to them in geography and culture. This strategy develops leadership for truly global ministry and empowers partner churches through fuller participation in that ministry. Likewise, the Board increasingly uses people from stricken areas in disaster relief and recovery efforts—in natural disasters as well as civil wars and social upheavals. This is good stewardship and affirms the contextual role of leadership.

The professional staff of the Board is becoming more diverse and reflective of our global UMC connection. Such diversity strengthens the Board and The UMC with the insights, experiences, and talents of women and men from every region of the earth. This is vital for a global agency with global responsibilities.

Discovery Church Journey

Barbara Greaves recalls that, on her first visit to a new UMC in Diamondhead, Mississippi, "'the people were so kind, I thought something was wrong with them.'"[5] The Diamondhead church, which grew from thirty-five to 150 members in five years, captures the spirit of Discovery Church Journey, an approach that moves a congregation from an inward to an outward focus. Discovery churches exist for their nonmembers. The goal is renewal, transformation, greater local and global outreach, and growth—all of which illustrate a commitment to action for the gospel.

Leadership Development

As part of its primary goal to make disciples for Jesus Christ, the Board held four academies for Evangelization and Church Growth in Africa. More than 170 people attended regional academies that underscored common issues facing the church across national boundaries. Similarly, training for church developers in Latin America included training for *asesores* (men) and *asesoras* (women) to accompany, or "walk with," emerging congregations. This program, which is carried out in partnership with the Methodist Council of Churches in Latin America and the Caribbean (CIEMAL), held events for new church starts in Honduras, El Salvador, Nicaragua, Colombia, and Venezuela and for older churches in Peru, Bolivia, and Argentina.

In Mission Together

More than 800 congregations in the U.S. are paired with congregations in Africa, Asia, Latin America, and eastern Europe for shared ministry and mission. This program also relates to other ministries, such as the Russia Initiative and the expanding church-growth efforts in Cambodia.

Mission Personnel

At the close of 2001, GBGM supported mission personnel in seventy-five countries around the world. Almost 2,200 served the gospel in ministries of evangelization, church development, education, agriculture, health and human services, relief and rehabilitation, and many combinations of these forms of Christian outreach.

The year 2001 marked the fiftieth anniversary of one of the most successful missionary initiatives in Methodism: the US-2 Program. Over the course of half a century, 1,171 young adults were commissioned for two-year mission assignments in the U.S.

Early in 2002 GBGM sent its first missionary to Mongolia. Helen Sheperd, who had worked as a missionary in Korea since 1992, went to Ulaanbaatar, the capital. She had previously visited Mongolia with a Korean Methodist team, part of the mission of the Korean Methodist Church, which established a medical clinic in Mongolia. She had also met Mongolian doctors when they came to Korea for medical training. Sheperd will first work as a nurse with a hospice program established by Yonsei University and Hospital, Republic of Korea. She will also seek a building that will serve as a mission center in Ulaanbaatar. Since there are an estimated 8,000 Christians in Mongolia, United Methodists will work with them in a common effort.

Seven men and women between the ages of eighteen and thirty from five countries were commissioned and sent in 2001 in the first class of Bishop W. T. Handy, Jr., Young Adult Missioners. The second class of Missioners of Hope was received. Forty-eight missioners, mostly young adults, were assigned exclusively to ministries with children in Africa.

Mission Volunteers

In 2001, United Methodist Volunteers in Mission (UMVIM) celebrated twenty-five years as a recognized United Methodist agency. Among these volunteers are Nomads on a Mission of Active Divine Service (NOMADS), a ministry with its own staff member and board of directors that provides intergenerational family summer projects as well as year-long projects for people with recreational vehicles and others. VIMs enable people of all ages and skills to participate in hands-on ministries in short-term mission projects. More than 171,000 youth and adults served as VIMs in the U.S. and seventy other countries during 2000 and 2001.

In Partnerships for the Full Gospel

The Board understands itself to be in a mutually supportive relationship with mission partners serving Christ's full mission. Whenever United Methodists are in mission, the Wesleyan concern for personal witness and social holiness guides our ministries. The agency is to "plan with others and to establish and strengthen Christian congregations where opportunities and needs are found" (*2000 Book of Discipline*, ¶1302.4). Correspondingly, the agency seeks partners in fulfilling the charge to "identify with all who are alienated and dispossessed and to assist them in achieving their full human development—body, mind, and spirit" (*2000 Book of Discipline*, ¶1302.11). The Board works collaboratively, and often ecumenically, on issues of social and economic justice, human rights, and advocacy for the full participation of women in church and society.

The 1990s formed the most active UMC mission decade of the twentieth century. As a result, United Methodism entered the twenty-first century with a large number of new churches around the world.

Bulgaria/Macedonia

In 2002 there were thirty congregations in this predominantly Eastern Orthodox country. It had six ordained pastors, one probationer, and a dozen lay pastors. Outreach and preaching, conducted in five languages, were directed particularly to minority populations, including the Romany (Gypsies). The Central Conference of Central and Southern Europe was in 2002 developing a program for the training of new pastors to serve Bulgaria, Yugoslavia, and Macedonia.

The Board missionary in Macedonia is a specialist in Christian education. The country was strongly affected by the flood of immigrants from Bosnia. Boris Trajkouvsi, president of Macedonia, is a United Methodist lay preacher.

Cambodia

After several congregations were started in the 1990s as the result of efforts by Cambodian refugee communities in the U.S. and Europe, the number of UMC churches grew to forty-four by early 2001. A year later the number of churches was more than one hundred. GBGM has published a hymnal in Khmer, the national language of Cambodia. In 2001 the Youth Mission Chorale—twenty-three college and university students—toured Asia, with stops in Cambodia as well as China, Indonesia, Malaysia, Mongolia, and Singapore. Global Praise publications include six CDs of missional and indigenous Christian music, three songbooks, and a hymnal for the church in Cambodia.

Cameroon

The first congregations of The UMC in Cameroon came about through the labors of Ayuk Enow, a layman who studied in the U.S. and returned to his homeland almost twenty years ago with the dream of introducing United Methodism. In 2000, a delegation from the Board visited with Ayuk Enow and other local leaders, bringing about a formal relationship with the agency. A regional missionary from the Women's Division, Catherine Akale, arrived in Yaoundé, the capital, in 2000; and in late 2001, two Board missionaries, both Africans, were assigned. According to a report in *New World Outlook:*

"While Ayuk continues working for the government, he serves as a lay pastor on the weekends in Buea, where he now lives. An additional lay pastor has assisted in Sumbe [another town where a United Methodist congregation is found], and a Baptist pastor... is assisting with two congregations."[6]

Guinea

The sixteen congregations in this West African country trace their roots to the mission work of Liberians who found refuge in Guinea from civil war in their country in the early 1990s. After many refugees returned in 1997, GBGM continued to nurture a United Methodist presence in this predominantly Muslim country. Missioners of Hope and other missionary personnel have been assigned here. The Guinean church today has one thousand members, a 550-student primary school, a rural clinic, a ministry to street children, and an agricultural mission.

Honduras

The UMC in Honduras is only five years old but has already launched twelve faith communities. Some of the church growth came from UMCOR efforts to rebuild homes in the wake of the 1998 hurricane. Some of the residents wanted to know who was helping with the rebuilding. When told they were United Methodists, the inquirers wanted to become a part of a faith community.

A key component of the Honduras initiative is the GBGM-sponsored schools of leadership development, where attendees are taught what it means to be a Christian and how to lead churches. They are also taught Methodist history and liturgy and preaching. The leadership school graduated its first class of students in March 2002. These graduates assumed leadership positions in the growing church.

In Mission Together

This program helps churches in different parts of the world engage in shared ministry and mission. By 2002, more than 800 congregations in the U.S. were paired with churches in Africa, Asia, Latin America, and eastern Europe. These were not one-way ministries but real partnerships that strengthen the spiritual, social, and service ministries of each partner.

Latvia / Lithuania

The church in Latvia at the end of 2001 had twelve congregations, a district superintendent, four ordained indigenous clergy, two local pastors, and four missionaries. Membership was one thousand within a community of 2,559. By 2002 there were nine congregations in Lithuania, a superintendent, and seven missionaries. Formal membership was 424 within a larger community of 1,100. Both churches have administrative councils and are part of the Northern European Central Conference.

Namibia

The UMC in Namibia is part of the West Angola Conference and by 2002 had ten thousand members, although it is only seven years old. It had several lay pastors but only one ordained clergy, the Reverend Ludwig Siyaka Hausiku. He is supported by the Board as an indigenous Person in Mission. He reported that he sometimes baptized one hundred believers at a time. Agriculture is a major priority, and the church provided corn and vegetable seeds to the San, or Bushmen, nomadic people whose hunting and gathering way of life is being threatened by expanding populations and wilderness preservation.

Russia

By 2002 there were some one hundred congregations across this vast land, from the southeast near Japan to St. Petersburg in the northwest. Almost all of the pastors were Russian. There were thirty-two ordained clergy, forty-two probationers, and nineteen candidates.

Senegal

By 2002, L'Eglise Methodiste Unie au Senegal (EMUS) was a registered church with eight congregations. Four pastors are Senegalese and four are from other parts of Africa. The EMUS is particularly concerned with maintaining cordial relations with Muslim neighbors and with other Christians.

Vietnam/Laos

No UMC, as such, actually exists in either Vietnam or Laos; but active explorations are under way, although the situations differ in each country. The greatest momentum has come from Vietnamese and Laotian United Methodist communities in the U.S. — clergy and church members who want to see United Methodism firmly planted in the lands of their origins. A Vietnamese Mission Initiative was set up in 2000, following a meeting in Ho Chi Minh City of Vietnamese pastors who wish to affiliate with The UMC. A Vietnamese edition of *Who Are the People Called Methodist?* has been published. The situation in Laos is less advanced. The Lao Evangelical Church is the one officially recognized Protestant denomination in the country.

Conclusion

With the whole world as our parish, GBGM seeks, on behalf of The UMC, to embody the Christian and Wesleyan conviction that all of life is within the promise of the saving, judging reign of God. All that the Board accomplishes and seeks to accomplish through its directors, staff, missionaries, and mission partners depends upon the constant prayers, voluntary participation, and generous gifts of millions of United Methodist women, men, young people, and children. With thanksgiving to God and appreciation for the support of the global United Methodist family, I celebrate our ministry together.

[Notes]

Pfisterer : A Journey of Amazing Grace

1. In The Methodist Church the division was titled "Woman's Division." In 1968 when The Methodist Church and the Evangelical United Brethren united to form The United Methodist Church, the title was changed to "Women's Division," the title used by Evangelical United Brethren.
2. The citation was read at the organizational meeting of the Women's Division, September 10, 1980. Original in author's possession.
3. Original release with this title from United Methodist News Service, by Tim Tanton, September 10, 1999.

    Pacific Homes was a United Methodist chain of fourteen retirement homes and convalescent hospitals in California, Arizona, and Hawaii. When the chain had financial problems, it filed for bankruptcy in 1977. When it asked residents for money beyond their contractual obligations, some of the residents filed lawsuits. Claims from the lawsuits came to nearly a half-billion dollars. The claims were against the former Pacific and Southwest Annual Conference, the General Council of Finance and Administration (GCFA), and the General Board of Global Ministries, all of The United Methodist Church. One of the issues was whether the entire denomination was liable, since Pacific Homes used the name of The UMC. The issue was never clarified because the lawsuits ended in settlements. Because of the suits, however, General Conference adopted legislation stating the denomination is not a "jural" entity capable of being sued. In addition, many annual conferences restated their relations with institutions they supported to avoid liability or clarify what their liability was.

    In the settlements, the successors to the Pacific and Southwest Conference (divided into the California-Pacific and Desert Southwest conferences) paid about $2 million, the GCFA about $4 million, and GBGM about $3 million. Payment of the settlement was structured as a loan to the conferences, which would receive money back if Pacific Homes recovered its financial stability. A partial repayment of $7.5 million was made in 1992 when the settlement was restructured. Another $16.4 million in 1999 retired the full amount of the loan. Ed.
4. I might add that following my eight-year term as a director, I applied for and was hired as a field staff member of the general Board and was assigned to the Office of Finance and Field Service, where I worked for almost twelve years. My decision was to become part of the solution, although there were a few women who had proved themselves many times over prior to my joining the staff.

    It is interesting, at least to me, to muse on the turns life takes. From a director who votes policy to be implemented by executive staff, I became a staff member of the Board assigned to an office supervised by the Congregational Development Program unit of the National Division. The division was in turn responsible to the directors and staff secretary who headed that unit, and ultimately to Dr. Randolph Nugent, the "big boss." That seems to me to make full circle!

5. In 2001 this profile summarizes major trends in membership giving for a United Methodist church for the past ten years and also charts population growth and lifestyle trends in the zip code community that surrounds the church. It is provided by the Research Office at GBGM, 475 Riverside Drive, New York, NY 10115.

Gordon : The Origin and Creation of a Theology of Mission Statement

1. These and other direct quotations are taken from documents in the author's possession. They can also be found in the *Daily Journal* of the General Board of Global Ministries in the spring or fall annual meetings on or just following the dates cited.
2. Three members of the task force had served in the preceding quadrennium: Bivens plus Ruth Daugherty, Pennsylvania, and Marilyn Winters, California. Members from the 1984 quadrennium, all Board directors, were Bishop Emerito P. Nacpil, the Philippines; Max Bailor, Sierra Leone; Tove Odland, Norway; Bishop Roy Sano, Denver Area; Tal Oden, Oklahoma; Betty S. Gordon, West Virginia; Jun Soon Bergmann, New York; Bishop Roy Clark, South Carolina; Dorothy Ravenhorst, Virginia; James Salley, South Carolina; John Stumbo, Kansas; the Reverend Sandra Hoke, Illinois; Zenobia Waters, Arkansas; and the Reverend Mary Ann Swenson, Washington. Dr. Nugent and Bishop James Ault, president of the Board, served ex officio.
3. Following is the "listening agenda" used at the consultations:
    1. What particular historical perspectives are needed to appreciate the development of the mission theology being discussed?
    2. The manner in which the culture, traditions, mores and values of this setting are reflected in the discussion of theological perspectives of mission (*sic*).
    3. What Biblical frames of reference for discussing the mission of the church was (*sic*) dominant in the discussion?
    4. What was the basic doctrinal theme upheld by the discussion of mission theology?
    5. What were the most compelling missional issues addressed?
    6. Identify as many perspectives on theology as were explicitly articulated in the presentations and discussions. Wesleyan Evangelical, Process, Liberation (Feminist, Black, Hispanic, Other).
    7. Which of the following agents of missional efforts were most clearly supported by the discussion? Sending Missionaries, Exchanging Missionaries, Proclaiming the Gospel, Advocating Social Change, Developing Churches, Other.
    8. What new vision for Global Mission did you discover in this consultation? Elaborate.

9. What documents or other expressions of the Word of God (or about God's acts) commend themselves for special consideration in the development of a contemporary global mission statement? Include copies of any documents or full description (pictures, tapes, journals, letters, music, drama, portraits, etc.) that will assist in sharing these important contributions to this consultation.

4. The Mission Convocation Committee met for the first time in February 1985, and its formal purposes were outlined as:
"To witness to our unity through faith in Jesus Christ
To discover new ways to equip ourselves for witness and evangelism
To share our theological understanding and to renew our Wesleyan enthusiasm
To accept the challenge of the new mission age
To learn from the church in mission."

5. The author served as interim associate general secretary of the Mission Personnel Resources Program Department in 1991.

Skeete : Years of Initiative for Mission

1. The *deaf* are those who are born deaf or become deaf in infancy. They are also known as the culturally deaf. The *deafened* are also called audiologically deaf. They are those who become deaf after language is established. The *hard-of-hearing* are those who have some residual hearing and may use hearing aids and other listening devices. They are referred to as the culturally hearing. "Report of the National Committee on Developing Deaf Ministry," *Daily Christian Advocate*, Advance edition, 1996 General Conference, p. 742.

Solomon : Mission Is Incarnation

1. The Bishop W.T. Handy, Jr., Young Adult Missioners program, named after a deceased UMC bishop, placed youth/young adults from every country in mission/service. It used the concept of "everywhere to everywhere" to send persons on short-term assignments from many countries, not merely the U.S., to other countries.

Kulah : Endowed by God

1. Cox's words have become part of the lore of the mission movement. Apparently this phrase first appeared in a diary that was published in Gershom F. Cox, *Remains of Melville B. Cox* (New York: Mason and Lane, 1840), noted in Wade Crawford Barclay, *Early American Methodism, 1769–1844* (New York: Methodist Board of Missions, 1949), 1: 330.

Bolleter : Developing a Culture of Mutuality

1. Mrs. Francesca Nast Gamble belonged to the Nast family mentioned here and was married to a member of the famous soap company. She gave large gifts for the support of mission of the MEC. In 1913 she gave $50,000 for a building in

Russia that would serve as Methodist headquarters there. This gift was part of a larger donation of $175,000 that was then the largest single gift by an individual in the history of the MEC Board of Missions. This larger donation comprised contributions also to Budapest, China, and a fund for the Board's administrative expenses. J. Tremayne Copplestone, *Twentieth-Century Perspectives: The Methodist Episcopal Church, 1896–1939* (New York: United Methodist Board of Global Ministries, 1973), pp. 83, 372, 377.

Gaither Warfield was the head of the Methodist Committee on Overseas Relief and helped to found and to support many of the orphanages and other social institutions in Central Europe, especially after the Second World War. From an e-mail of Heinrich Bolleter, July 24, 2002.

2. Wilhelm Nausner, *The Geneva Area: A Short History of a Branch of The United Methodist Church in Europe* (Zurich: CVB Buch and Druck, 1976), p. 9.
3. Nausner, *The Geneva Area*, p. 21.

Fernandez : Visions Shaping the Future

1. The United Methodist Church refers to its conferences outside the U.S. that are supported as missions as "central conferences." These conferences are amenable to the General Conference. Methodist or United Methodist churches that choose independence become "autonomous churches," which means they are no longer amenable to General Conference of The UMC, although they may continue to receive mission support. In the late 1960s, the Latin American churches who were part of the former Methodist Church became autonomous.
2. Cox, *Fire from Heaven: The Rise of Pentecostal Spirituality and the Reshaping of Religion in the 21st Century* (Boston: Addison-Wesley, 1995), pp. 182, 276–277.

Yeoh : Witnessing to the Gospel in Word and Deed

1. The Medicine Box program enables churches and service organizations to contribute partial quantities of essential items, in the form of a kit of over-the-counter products and supplies. American pharmaceutical companies provide numerous medications needed for the Medicine Box through donations or discounted pricing. The distribution of the boxes is done through Interchurch Medical Assistance.

The UMCOR Depot, located at a Women's Division school, Sager-Brown in Baldwin, Louisiana, is formally known as the Sager-Brown Warehouse for Churchwide Disaster Relief.

The depot, which is the size of two football fields, is supplied by UMW and churches around the country, who compile kits of relief supplies and other aid and send them to the depot for storage. These supplies are then sent to disaster areas when there is need.

2. Jane Dennis, "New Center to Train Students for Health Care Careers," United Methodist News Service release, Nov. 21, 2001.

Pagura : Fifty Years after the Universal Declaration of Human Rights

1. Enrique Angelelli was a Roman Catholic priest in La Rioja, Argentina, where his pastoral ministry made him beloved by the poor. He was threatened several times with death because of his advocacy of justice for the poor. Later, as a bishop in Córdoba, Argentina, "He had a clear engagement with the poor, was counted among the most progressive bishops in Latin America, and was clearly related to Third World Liberation Theology." In August 1976, when Argentina was ruled by a military dictatorship, he and a companion, a Father Pinto, were involved in a car accident. Pinto testified afterward that the car in which they were riding was pushed to the side of the road by a truck, and when he became conscious, Msgr. Angelelli was dead by his side. Police came and buried the body without an autopsy. The official cause of death was that he was killed in the car accident. Many believe Angelelli survived the accident and was then killed while unconscious. There was an investigation in 2001, but the judge ruled that it was impossible to establish the cause of death because of the lack of evidence. Also in 2001 there was a commemoration of the twenty-fifth anniversary of Angelelli's death. Many in La Rioja and elsewhere consider him a martyred saint. Information and quotation from Néstor O. Miguez, a Methodist pastor in Buenos Aires, to the editor, June 25, 2001.
2. This and the preceding quotation come from *Agencia Latinoamericana de Información*, no. 275, June 30, 1998, Quito, Ecuador.
3. "Unity Testimony," page 14, item 6, Consejo Latinoamericano de Iglesias [CLAI], Quito, Ecuador.
4. "Guía de trabajo de la Asamblea" ("Assembly Work Guide"), p. 71.
5. Buenos Aires *Clarin*, July 25, 1998.
6. "La Religión, La Exclusión y La Teología," Buenos Aires *Página 12*, July 14, 1996.
7. "Unity Testimony," page 4, item 45.

Martinez : Mission: A Commitment to Action

1. Much of this report is taken from "Mission: A Commitment to Action," the 2000–2001 biennial report of GBGM, published in July 2002, but important updates have been added from *New World Outlook* and other sources. Acknowledgment is made to Elliott Wright, a Board consultant, for his assistance in writing the biennial report.
2. This and the preceding quotations come from *New World Outlook* 92 (July/August 2002): 12–15.
3. *New World Outlook* 92 (July/August 2002): 18.
4. Paul Jeffrey, "Churches Help Make Peace a Reality in Post-War Angola," United Methodist News release, July 29, 2002.
5. "Mission: A Commitment to Action," p. 14.
6. *New World Outlook* 92 (July/August 2002): 10.

[Permissions]

Used with permission of the General Commission on Archives and History, the United Methodist Church: Photo of J. Edward Carothers, p. 15.

Used with permission of United Methodist Communications: Photos of Cambodia, p. 67; Angola mine victims, p. 69; Tallinn Center, p. 86; Honduras relief, p. 99; Zambia health worker, p. 103; and Ground Zero, p. 115.

All other photos in text and on cover are the property of the General Board of Global Ministries, The United Methodist Church.

[Index]

Abuelas of Argentina: photo, 109.
Action by Churches Together (ACT): in Angola, 118–119; in the Balkans, 68.
Advance for Christ and His Church: and aid after Oklahoma City bombing, 59; and Hope for Children of Africa, 69; and 1989–1990 projects, 53; mentioned, 61–62, 89.
Affirmation, as United Methodist caucus: 31.
Afghanistan: 65, 114, 115.
Africa: and addiction, 116; and church growth, 56; and health ministries, 115; and Liberia, 75–80; and Mozambique conflict, 50–53; and regional missionaries, 119–120; and regional presence, 92; and relief, 57, 115; as site of consultation, 27–28; and theology issues, 32; mentioned, 122. *See also* Millennium Fund for Mission, names of countries.
Africa Church Growth and Development: contribution of during 1980s, 52–53; and bishops, 79; and Mozambique, 50; and relation to Europe, 86; mentioned, 57.
Africa University: 4–5, 76.
African Americans: and education for doctors, 104–105; as Kendall Fund recipients, 102–104; and need for church to relate to differently, 92; as objects of violence, 66; and racial conflict, 18; mentioned, 36.
AIDS: in the DRC, 117; and Interagency Task Force, 60–61; Nugent's work for, 54; mentioned, 71, 116.
Alaska Missionary Conference: 24, 55.
Alves, Rubén: 107.
Angelelli, Enrique: 108 *n1*.
Angola: 68, 76, 118. *See also* photo, 69.
Argentina: 110, 122. *See also* photo, 109.
Arole, Raj and Mabel: 70.
Asia: and dialogue for women, 120; and health ministries, 115; and new churches, 58 ; omitted from Millennium Fund, 96; and regional missionaries, 119–120; as site of consultation, 27–28; and theology issues, 32; mentioned, 122. *See also* names of countries.

Asian-American Language Ministry: 61.
Austria: 83, 85, 87.
Autonomous churches: 92 *n1*.
Azerbaijan: 65.

Balkans: 82. *See also* Bosnia, Bulgaria, Croatia, Kosovo, Macedonia.
Baltics: 82, 83. *See also* Estonia, Latvia, Lithuania.
Baltimore-Washington Conference: 116.
Belgium: 82.
Belize: 115.
Bideaux, René: 19.
Bivens, C. Rex: 27.
Black caucus: 19.
Black community developers: 19.
Boff, Leonardo: 110.
Bolivia: 93, 94, 97–98, 122.
Bonino, Míguez: 107.
Bosnia: and immigrants in, 124; and mission personnel in, 66, 68; and relief work, 59; mentioned, 85.
Botswana: 65.
Brazil: 89, 110.
British Methodists: 82.
Bulgaria: 66, 83, 84, 124.
Burundi: 57, 65, 68, 77.

California-Nevada Conference: 92.
Cambodia: and church growth, 122, 124; and facilitating mission, 91; and mission education, 116; and new UM presence in, 64; mentioned, 58. *See also* photo, 67.
Cameroon: 120, 124–125.
Caribbean: 32. *See also* names of countries.
Carothers, J. Edward: 13–14. *See also* photo, 15.
Central America: *See* Latin America, names of countries.
Central Conference of Central and Southern Europe: 83–84, 124.
Central Conference of Central Europe: 82–83.
Central conferences: 92 *n1*.

[137]

Children and poverty: 69.
Church Center for United Nations: 52.
CIEMAL: 93, 122.
CLAI: 109–110.
Colombia: 58, 64, 122.
Communication: and dialogue with annual conferences, 55, 72–73; and indigenous resources, 116; as interpretation to local church, 22, 96–97; through print, 72, 116; through radio, 72, 116; of United Methodist News Service, 26; through video, 72; through world wide web, 72.
Communities of Shalom: 60, 70, 115–116.
Community health care: 70, 115.
Consultations: in Africa, 77; in Europe on end of Cold War, 85; to gather data for Theology of Mission Statement: 28–30. *See also* photo, 29.
Contextualization: 27, 32, 92, 93–95.
Costa Rica: and regional missionaries, 120; as site of consultation, 28, 29; and women's gathering, 120; mentioned, 29, 30, 37.
Cox, Harvey: 95, 97.
Cox, Melville: 76 *n1*.
Croatia: 68.
Cuba: 115.
Czech and Slovak republics: 65, 87.
Czechoslovakia: 82.

Deaconesses: 66.
Deaf ministry: 61 *n1*.
Democratic Republic of the Congo: 57, 68, 76, 117.
Denmark: 82.
Dharmaraj, Glory and Jacob: 117.
Discovery Church Journey: 122.
Domingos, Gaspar: 118.

Eastern Europe: 56. *See also* Russia Initiative.
Education: *See* mission education.
El Salvador: 64, 65, 115, 122.
Emory University: 49.
Enow, Ayuk: 124–125.
Estonia: 57, 116. *See also* photo, 86.
Ethnic Minority Local Church: 18, 21
Europe: 81–87, 116. *See also* Russia Initiative, names of countries.
European Commission on Mission: 86.
Evangelical Association: 82, 84.
Evangelization: in Africa, 77, 122; as issue for theology, 32; in Latin America, 122; and new congregations globally, 64–65; in Russia, 48.
Ewha University: 120.

Fama, Onema: 36, 117.
Felder, Cain: 32–34.
Finance and Field Service (office of): 18 *n4*.
Finland: 82.
France: 82, 84.

Gamble-Nast, Fannie: 82 *n1*.
Garber, Paul N.: 83.
General Board of Discipleship: 117.
General Board of Higher Education and Ministry: 4, 85.
General Board of Pensions: 79.
General Council on Ministries: 14–15.
Georgia, Republic of: 65.
German Evangelical and Brethren churches: 84.
German Methodist Church: 29–30, 81, 83, 87.
Ghana: 116, 120.
Giudice, Alberto: 108.
Global Gatherings: and first held in Louisville, 36–37; and inception, 30–31; in Indianapolis, 62.
Good News caucus: 12, 31
Gorbazova, Ludmilla: 48.
Ground Zero: photo, 115.
Guinea: 65, 125.
Gulfside Assembly: 104.
Gutiérrez, Gustavo: 107.
Gutiérrez, Isaías, 36.

Haines, Harry: 14.
Haiti: 116.
Handy, Bishop W. T., Jr., Young Adult Missioners: 66 *n1*, 123.
Hate and violence: 59, 66–67.
Hausiku, Ludwig Siyaka: 126.
Health and Welfare Ministries: 12–13, 102–104, 114, 115.
Hispanics: *See* MARCHA, National Plan for Hispanic Ministry, Rio Grande Conference.
HIV/AIDS: *See* AIDS.
Homelessness: 60.
Homosexuality: 20.
Honduras: and initiative from indigenous people, 91; and launching of faith communities, 125; and new presence in 1997–2000, 64, 65; and partnership with CIEMAL, 122. *See also* photo, 99.
Hope for Children of Africa: 69.
Human rights: 107–111, 118, 124.
Humper, Joseph: 77.
Hungary: 65, 83, 87.

Iglesia Evangelica Metodista Boliviana: 93.
India: 70, 115.
Indigenous Community Developers: 52.
Indigenous missionaries: 121.
Indonesia: 65, 124.
In Mission Together program, 126.
Interreligious Foundation for Community Organization: 4.

Jamaica: 28, 109, 111.
Jones, Tracey K., Jr.: 3, 8–9, 14.

Kaliningrad: 65.
Kazakhstan: 57, 65, 66, 91.
Kendall Fund Committee: 102–104.
Kenya: 65, 120.
Korean-American missionaries: 66.
Korean Methodist Church: 16–17, 120, 123.
Kosovo: 68, 85, 114.
Kulah, Arthur: photo, 78.

Land mines: 68, 114, 117–118. *See also* photo, 69.
Laos: 58, 65, 127.
Latin America: and council of churches, 93; and health ministries, 115; and human rights, 107–111; and Latin America/Caribbean Region office, 90, 92; and new churches, 58; omitted from Millennium Fund, 96; and regional missionaries, 119–120; as site of consultation, 27; and theology issues, 32; and women's gathering, 120; mentioned, 22, 122. *See also* names of countries.
Latvia: 56, 116, 126.
Liberation Theology: 107, 109.
Liberia: and hospital in Ganta, 114; and origin of Methodist mission, 75–76; mentioned, 125.
Lithuania: and missionaries assigned to, 65, 66; and mission education, 116; and new presence in, 64; and reorganization of oldest church in Russian Empire, 56; and size of church, 126.
Louisiana Annual Conference, 43.

Macedonia: 85, 124.
Machado, Joab: 77.
Malawi: 65.
Malaysia: home of Jennie Yeoh, 101; and mission by invitation, 105; and UMW Bible Women's Pilot project, 120; mentioned, 65, 124.
Malik, Charles: 107.

Mandela, Nelson: 110.
MARCHA: 31, 94.
Medical missions: in Angola, 118; in Chernobyl, 44; in Kazakhstan, 57, 91; in Moscow, 44; in Mozambique, 50–52. *See also* AIDS, community health care, Health and Welfare Ministries.
Medicine Boxes: 53, 102, 103, 115.
Meharry Medical College: 104.
Memphis: 28, 30.
Methodist Church: 83–84.
Methodist Episcopal Church: 82–83.
Methodist Episcopal Church, South: 82.
Methodist Federation for Social Action: 31.
Mexico: 110.
Millennium Fund for Mission: 71, 79, 87, 95–96.
Missionaries: number of, 66, 122. *See also* Handy, W. T., Jr., Young Adult Missioners, Missioners of Hope, US-2.
Mission convocation: *See* Global Gatherings.
Mission Development Committee: 95, 98.
Mission education: 56, 77–78.
Missioners of Hope: creation of, 66; as empowering in Africa, 79; as example of facilitating mission, 91; in Guinea, 125; second class of, 123.
Mission Evangelism Committee: 90, 102.
Mission Resource Center: 48–50.
Mission Society for United Methodists: 31.
Mission statement: 10. *See also* 25–38.
Mission volunteers: *See* Volunteers in Mission.
Mongolia: 123, 124.
Moore, Arthur J.: 83.
Mozambique: and Africa Church Growth and Development, 50; and hospital at Chicuque, 50–52; and land mines, 68, 114; mentioned, 76, 77. *See also* photo, 53.
Mutuality in Mission: 117.
Muzorewa, Abel: 77.
Myanmar: 65.

Namibia: 65, 126.
Nast, William: 81.
National Division: 3, 7–24. *See also* photo, 15.
National Federation for Asia American United Methodists: 31.
National Mission Institutions: 116.
National Plan for Hispanic Ministry: 60, 90, 92.
National Plan for Town and Country Ministries: 116.

Native Americans: and Native American Comprehensive Plan, 61; and Oklahoma Indian Missionary Conference, 23–24, 55; mentioned, 92.
Ndoricimpa, Alfred: 77.
Nepal: 65.
New Guinea: 66.
New World Outlook: 72.
New York Conference: 114.
Nicaragua: 58, 65.
Nigeria: 120.
Northern European Central Conference, 126.
North Korea: 115.
Norway: 82.
Nuelsen, John L.: 82–83.
Nugent, Randolph W.: and Africa American Association, 53; and AIDS benefit, 54; background of, 1–3; and call to review GBGM theology, 26; and comments on mission convocation, 31; and contributions to mission in Africa, 76–79; as dedicated to mission, 64; as first African-American head of GBGM, 1; as general secretary of GBGM, 13, 14, 15, 25; as head of National Division, 4, 10; and name given to Mission Center at Philander Smith College, 104; and peacebuilding in the DRC, 117; and Russia Initiative, 39–48, 90–91; and support of Africa University, 4; and support of Europe mission, 87; and support of theology of mission, 38; mentioned, 18 *n4*, 20, 30, 55, 75, 80, 99, 105–106. *See also* photo, xiv.

Oklahoma Indian Missionary Conference: 23–24, 55.
Oknah Kim Lah: 16–17.
Oregon-Idaho Conference: 90.

Pacific Homes: 12–13 *n3*.
Palestine: 66, 115, 120.
Partnership: in Africa, 76–77; with annual conferences, 55; in Bolivia, 92–93; in mission, 12, 35–36, 117, 123–124; through In Mission Together, 125.
Pensions: 79.
Peru: 97, 107, 122.
Philander Smith College: 104.
Philippines: dialogue with, 55; and regional missionaries, 120; and training for health care, 70; and volunteers in, 22.
Poland: 43, 82, 84, 87.

Quipungo, José and Laura Vidal: 118.

Red Bird Missionary Conference: 24, 55.
Refugees: in DRC and eastern Africa, 68; and resettlement of, 114; in West Africa, 125. *See also* photo, 58.
Research and Development Committee: 10, 19, 26, 31.
Response: 72.
Restorative Justice: 67.
Rio Grande Conference: 55, 96.
Romania: 65.
Rural chaplains: 59, 70.
Russia: in central conference, 83; and MEC, 82; and number of congregations, 126.
Russia Initiative : 39–48, 66, 90–91, 122. *See also* photo, 44.
Russian Orthodox Church: 40–42, 46–47, 56.
Rwanda: 57, 65, 68.

Sager-Brown Warehouse for Churchwide Disaster Relief: 102 *n1*.
Schnatz, Johann: 82.
Segundo, Juan Luis: 109.
Semipalatinsk: 57.
Senegal: and development of indigenous resources, 116; and 1995 mission establishment, 65; as recipient of new missionaries, 66; and regional missionaries, 120; as registered church, 126.
September 11, 2001, events: 114. *See also* photo, 115.
Serbia: 85. *See also* Balkans, Yugoslavia.
Shalom zones: *See* Communities of Shalom.
Siberia: 82.
Sierra Leone: 77.
Southwest Border Consultation: 23.
Soviet Union: *See* Russia, Russia Initiative.
Special Program on Substance Abuse and Related Violence: 116.
Structure: of GBGM, 5–6, 70–71, 91–92, 95–96.
Substance abuse: 60, 116.
Sudan: 65.
Sweden: 82.
Switzerland: and assistance to other churches, 87; and consultation, 25, 28; and EUB, 84; as part of MEC, 83.

Tanzania: 66.
Taylor, William: 76.
Teitelbaum, Alejandro: 108.
Texas Conference: 116.

Thailand: 58.
Theology of Mission Statement: 25–38. *See also* photo, 29.
Turkey: 115.
Tutu, Desmond: 36.

Uganda: 65, 66.
Ukraine: 65.
United Brethren: 82, 84.
United Methodist Committee on Relief: and disaster relief, 59, 62, 67–68, 105, 114–115; in Lithuania, 65; and Louisiana depot, 102, 115; and relation to conferences, 12; and response to September 11 events, 114; mentioned, 14, 98. *See also* photos, 99, 103.
United Methodist Development Fund: 71.
United Methodist Women: Ann Pfisterer as member of, 8, 9–10; Betty S. Gordon as member of, 38; centennial, 52; and communication, 72; and hate crimes, 59, 67; and homosexuality, 20; Jennie Yeoh as member of, 102; and language study, 85–86; and ministries with women, children, and youth, 90; and missionary in Cameroon, 124; and National Gathering of Teen and College/University Women, 120; and 1994 assembly, 62; and 1964 agreements, 8, 21, 52; and property of, 21; and regional missionaries, 120; and 2002 assembly, 120; and UMCOR depot, 102 n1; and welfare, 69, 116, 120; and women societies of foreign mission, 82; and Women's Division title, 8 n1; mentioned, 99, 101. *See also* photo, 121.

Universal Declaration of Human Rights: 107–111.
US-2: 122.

Venezuela: and initiative from indigenous area, 91; and new churches, 58, 64, 65, 122.
Vietnam: 58, 127.
Volunteers in Mission: 22–23, 56, 71, 114.

W. T. Handy, Jr.: 66 n1, 123.
Ward, Ralph: 17.
Warfield, Gaither: 82 n1.
Welfare: 68–69.
Wertz, Frederick: 9.
West Angola Conference: 126.
White, Woodie: 18
Women societies of foreign mission: 82.
Women's Division: *See* United Methodist Women.
World Council of Churches: 107–111, 117.
World Program Division: and new area office for Russia, 57; as problematic for Good News movement, 12; Solomon as member of, 63–64; mentioned, 52, 90.

Yeltsin, Naina: 46–47.
Yugoslavia: 82, 85, 87. *See also* names of countries.

Zaire: *See* Democratic Republic of the Congo.
Zambia: 53, 66. *See also* photo, 103.
Zimbabwe: 76, 77, 116.

Please mail order with check payable to:
SERVICE CENTER
7820 READING ROAD CALLER NO 1800
CINCINNATI OH 45222-1800

Costs for shipping and handling for sale items:
$25 or less, add $4.65
$25.01–$60, add $5.75
$60.01–$100, add $7.00
Over $100, add 6.5%

For billed and credit card orders:
CALL TOLL FREE: 1-800-305-9857
FAX ORDERS: 1-513-761-3722
E-MAIL: SCorders@gbgm-umc.org
If billing is requested, a $1.50 billing fee will be added.

$ 14.95 PAPERBACK	STOCK #03274
$ 21.95 HARDBACK	STOCK #02882